PRESENTED TO:

_____

FROM:

_____

DATE:

_____

HOPE FOR EACH DAY

365 DEVOTIONS FOR KIDS

BY BILLY GRAHAM

Adapted by Diane Stortz

A Division of Thomas Nelson Publishers

Published in Nashville, Tennessee, by Tommy Nelson. Tommy Nelson is an imprint of Thomas Nelson. Thomas Nelson is a registered trademark of HarperCollins Christian Publishing, Inc.

Cover designed by Left Coast Design.

Tommy Nelson titles may be purchased in bulk for educational, business, fund-raising, or sales promotional use. For information, please e-mail SpecialMarkets@ThomasNelson.com.

ISBN-13: 978-0-7180-8617-6
Library of Congress Cataloging-in-Publication Data is on file.

Printed in China

17 18 19 20 21 DSC 6 5 4 3 2

Mfr: RR Donnelley Asia / Shenzhen, China / May 2017 / PO #9442699

Therefore I live for today—
Certain of finding at sunrise
Guidance and strength for the way.
Power for each moment of weakness,
Hope for each moment of pain,
Comfort for every sorrow,
Sunshine and joy after rain!
—Anonymous

PREFACE

For many years I have sought to walk with God every day. What a joy it is to wake up in the morning and know He is with me, no matter what the day has in store. What a joy it is to look back in the evening and be able to thank Him for His faithfulness and to experience His peace. What a joy it is to know that someday soon the burdens of this life will be over and I will awaken in His presence!

When I think about God's love, I tend to dwell upon all the good things He has done for me. But then I must stop and realize that even when circumstances have been hard or the way unclear, God has still surrounded me with His love. God's love is just as real and just as powerful in the darkness as it is in the light. And that is why we can have hope!

Every day I turn to the Bible to give me strength and wisdom for the day and hope for the future. Its words have seen me through good times and bad—through times of happiness and grief, health and sickness, victory and disappointment. God's Word can do the same for you.

May God use these daily selections to encourage you and give you hope. May they also challenge you both to live more fully for Christ each day and to trust His great love—no matter what comes your way.

—Billy Graham

JANUARY

May the God of hope fill you with all joy.
ROMANS 15:13

IN TUNE WITH THE MASTER

You shall surround me with songs of deliverance.
PSALM 32:7

D o you like to listen to music? When singers sing the right notes and stay in tune, it is very beautiful. But when a singer does not sing the right notes, his voice does not blend with the others, and it doesn't sound very good. All the singers have to follow the notes assigned to them in the music and sing in tune for the music to sound as good as possible.

When we don't follow God's ways for our lives, we get out of tune—out of harmony with others and with God. It doesn't sound good to anyone. We hear words of anger, or selfishness, or unhappiness. But if we follow God's way—like the singers who follow their notes—our lives will be much happier, and we will find ourselves surrounded by His beautiful music.

As this new year begins, ask God to help you tune your life every day to His Word, the Bible, so you can bring harmony and joy to those around you.

THE SUN STILL SHINES

They looked . . . and behold, the glory of the Lord appeared in the cloud.
EXODUS 16:10

Everyone loves a sunny day, but we need cloudy days too. Without clouds there would be no rain to help plants grow. And without rain there would be no water. But after the rain, there is a beautiful rainbow and a bright sunny sky.

Sometimes we feel sad on cloudy days. But above the clouds the sky is blue and the sun is shining!

Problems can be like clouds. When trouble comes, we get worried. We forget that just as the sun is still shining above the clouds, God is still with us when we face problems. And He can turn our problems into blessings! When God led His people out of Egypt and through the wilderness, He led them by a cloud!

Sometimes our problems are small like white, fluffy clouds. Sometimes they are big and scary like big thunderstorm clouds. When you are worried or afraid, ask Jesus to help you. On happy, sunny days and on cloudy, worried days, God is right there with you, holding your hand and keeping you safe with Him.

JANUARY 3

HOW TO BE HAPPY

With You is the fountain of life.
PSALM 36:9

What makes you happy—winning a game? Getting a good grade? Riding a roller coaster?

We all feel happy when good things happen. But can we be happy even when bad things happen?

Peace is a special kind of happiness. Jesus promised peace to everyone who trusts and follows Him: "The water I give will become a spring of water flowing inside. . . . It will give [you] eternal life. . . . My peace I give you" (John 4:14, 14:27 ICB). Jesus' peace is like a natural spring— underground water that comes up through an opening in the earth.

Near my home is a spring that never stops flowing, no matter the weather. That is just like Jesus' peace. We can feel the peace Jesus gives us even when bad things happen.

So when you face a problem, remember to tell Jesus all about it and ask Him for His peace.

THE PROMISE IS OURS

"I am with you always, even to the end of the age."
MATTHEW 28:20

David Livingstone was a missionary and explorer in Africa. There were many adventures, but it was also very hard. After sixteen long years David returned to his home in Scotland for a visit. He was skinny and weak because he had been sick so often. His left arm had been mangled by a lion and hung useless at his side.

Speaking to university students, Livingstone said, "Shall I tell you what kept me going during the hard and lonely times? It was Jesus' promise, 'I am with you always, even to the end of the age.'"

That promise is ours too! No matter where we go—from our home to a faraway place like Africa—Jesus never leaves us. He is with us on our most exciting adventures and in our hardest days. Isn't it good to know that we have a God who loves us so much He never leaves us all on our own?

JANUARY 5

HERE TO HELP

Who shall separate us from the love of Christ?
ROMANS 8:35

At the empty tomb after Jesus' resurrection, women heard an angel say that Jesus was alive. And as they ran to tell His disciples the news, Jesus came to them and said, "Don't be afraid. Go and tell my brothers to go on to Galilee. They will see me there" (Matthew 28:10 ICB). Jerusalem was a dangerous place for Jesus' followers, but Jesus said, "Don't be afraid."

Jesus still comes to all who love Him and says, "Don't be afraid."

He comes when you are sick. He comes when you fail a test or when you are cut from the team. He comes when scary things happen or when people are mean to you. And He says, "Don't be afraid. I'm alive, and I'm here to help you. The cross shows the depth of My love, and the resurrection shows the depth of My power. Nothing can ever separate you from Me!"

MANY MANSIONS

"In My Father's house are many mansions. . . .
I go to prepare a place for you."
JOHN 14:2

There was once a little boy who was riding alone on a train, and the scenery was not too interesting. A woman sitting beside him asked, "Are you tired of the long ride?"

The boy smiled and said, "I'm a little tired, but I don't mind it much. You see, my father is going to meet me when I get there."

Just like that boy looked forward to having his father meet him at his destination, Christians look forward to having Jesus meet us when we arrive at our destination—Heaven! Jesus said, "I go to prepare a place for you."

You are young and have many wonderful years of life ahead of you. You have so many things to look forward to! But someday you will be old, and your life on earth will end.

Knowing that Jesus will meet us at the end of our life's journey takes any worry away. Paul wrote, "Therefore we do not lose heart. . . . For the things which are seen are temporary, but the things which are not seen are eternal" (2 Corinthians 4:16, 18). Our problems shrink when we remember we will be with Jesus forever!

BE THANKFUL

I have learned the secret of being content in any and every situation.
PHILIPPIANS 4:12 NIV

Some years ago I visited a man who was wealthy and successful. But as we talked, he broke down in tears. He confessed that while he looked happy on the outside, he was actually unhappy and miserable.

A few hours later I visited another man who lived only a few miles away. His cottage was humble, and he had very little. He told me about the work he was doing for Jesus and how Jesus filled his life with meaning and purpose. All over the world, when people learn about Jesus, they are so happy it is like their faces shine.

I went away convinced that the second man was really the rich man. Although he owned very little, he had learned to be thankful for everything God had given him. Being thankful makes all the difference.

GOD'S ERASER

"I—yes, I alone—will blot out your sins for my own sake."
ISAIAH 43:25 NLT

I f you are solving a math problem and you write down the wrong answer, what do you do? You get an eraser, remove the error, and start over, right? By erasing what you did wrong, it allows you to do the math problem again and do it correctly. That is how it is with God when we sin. God says, "I—yes, I alone—will blot out your sins for my own sake and will never think of them again" (Isaiah 43:25 NLT). God is willing to erase our sins and never call them to mind again! It is like He has an eraser that takes away the bad things we did (our sins) and allows us to start over fresh and clean. This is wonderful news, and it applies to all people, everywhere—including you.

Have you received God's gift of forgiveness? If you have, thank Him for it—and if not, by faith invite Jesus into your life today.

JANUARY 9

BEAUTIFUL HANDS

He purchased our freedom with the blood of his Son.
EPHESIANS 1:7 NLT

A loving mother saved her baby girl from a burning house but badly burned her own hands. When the girl grew older, not knowing how her mother got those burns, she was ashamed of the ugly scars on her mother's hands and sometimes asked her to hide them.

But one day the daughter asked her mother, "What happened to your hands?" and her mother told her the story for the first time. The daughter cried tears of thanks and said, "Oh, Mama, those are beautiful hands, the most beautiful in the world. Don't ever hide them again!"

Jesus' scars and His death on the cross may seem ugly until we understand their importance. Because His blood rescued us from sin, Jesus' nail-pierced hands are beautiful beyond measure. They tell us of His love and His willingness to save us no matter the cost.

WHAT TO DO FIRST

"Seek first the kingdom of God."
MATTHEW 6:33

Have you ever watched a dog run in a circle, chasing its tail? Puppies do this a lot, but older dogs do it too. Sometimes it's just for fun and makes us laugh, but other times these dogs feel anxious. They're running in circles because they are afraid and don't know what to do.

People often think the way to be happy is to run around trying to find all the things that make them happy. But that is not the best way! True happiness comes a different way. Jesus told His disciples, "The thing you should want most is God's kingdom and doing what God wants. Then all these other things you need will be given to you" (Matthew 6:33 ICB). The "other things" He spoke of are the basic needs of life, like food, clothes, and a place to live. Jesus told us not to chase happiness, always running after what we want and what we need, but to "seek . . . the kingdom" first instead.

That, if we will accept it, is the secret of happiness: "Seek first the kingdom of God." How do we do this? By following King Jesus every day of our lives! This is the path of true happiness.

JANUARY 11

SHINE YOUR LIGHT

"You are the light of the world."
MATTHEW 5:14

Have you ever seen a flash mob? At a mall or in a big park, people come out of the crowd one by one to join in a dance or a song. The event has been planned ahead of time, but it doesn't look planned. At first the other shoppers or park visitors don't realize what's happening. But as the flash mob gets bigger, they can't help but notice!

Jesus said, "You should be a light for other people. Live so that they will see the good things you do. Live so that they will praise your Father in heaven" (Matthew 5:16 ICB). When we live like people who love Jesus, our little light can turn into a flame, lighting up the room when we live for Jesus. People see us living for Jesus, and they want to live for Him too.

So be that one light in the darkness! Live for Jesus—by the life you live and the words you speak.

JUST LIKE JESUS

We are in Him who is true, in His Son Jesus Christ.

1 JOHN 5:20

In the novel *In His Steps* by Charles M. Sheldon, a pastor challenges the people in his church. He asks them to promise for one year not to do anything without first asking the question, "What would Jesus do?"

That's a very good question to ask ourselves every day! Whatever is happening, Jesus knows what to do.

In the book, the pastor's challenge began after a poorly dressed man, whose wife had died, walked into a wealthy church and spoke to the congregation. He said, "I heard some people singing at a church prayer meeting the other night: 'All for Jesus! All for Jesus! All my being's ransomed powers; all my thoughts and words and doings, all my days and all my hours.'" The man continued, "I kept wondering as I sat on the steps outside just what they meant by it. It seems to me there's an awful lot of trouble in the world that somehow wouldn't exist if all the people who sing such songs went and lived them out."

If someone said those words to us, how would we respond? Do we live our lives with the thought *What would Jesus do?* and put it into practice every day?

GOD'S BLESSINGS

Every good gift and every perfect gift is from above.
JAMES 1:17

I n the Lord's Prayer are these familiar words: "Give us this day our daily bread" (Matthew 6:11). They remind us that we depend on God for everything, even what we eat each day. God is the Giver of every blessing: "Every good gift and every perfect gift is from above, and comes down from the Father of lights" (James 1:17).

You might wonder, *Why should I pray for my daily bread? My parents give me everything I need.* But listen: If it weren't for God's love and grace, we wouldn't have anything. We *all* need to pray this prayer every day, because we all need to be reminded to trust God in everything.

This prayer reminds us also of Jesus' words, "I am the bread of life. He who comes to Me shall never hunger" (John 6:35). Thank God for all His gifts—especially Christ, the greatest Gift of all.

JESUS IS THE CURE

If anyone is in Christ, he is a new creation.
2 CORINTHIANS 5:17

Before the first antibiotic, penicillin, was developed, diseases like pneumonia, strep throat, scarlet fever, and even tonsillitis frequently killed people. But with the use of penicillin, those diseases and many others could be treated and cured.

Wouldn't it be wonderful if we could also find a medicine to treat and cure all the problems we experience? Do you ever feel jealous or want your own way? Yes, we all do. Do you ever get angry and argue with others? Do you ever say hurtful things you don't mean? Suppose a cure could be found for these and all other problems.

The most thrilling news in the world is that there *is* a cure! God has provided the medicine—and that "medicine" is Jesus. Through Him our sins can be forgiven, and by His Holy Spirit within us our lives can be changed, made new, and made better.

This cure was provided two thousand years ago by Jesus' death and resurrection for us. We can have peace that doesn't depend on what is happening around us. Is He working daily in your life, changing you and making you more like Him?

JANUARY 15

LOOKING FOR LASTING JOY

May the God of hope fill you with all joy.
ROMANS 15:13

Did you ever get something you had wanted for a long time and thought would make you happy? Maybe it was a new outfit, a game, concert tickets, or a skateboard. How long did your happiness last? How long was it before there was something *else* you wanted and thought would make you happy? I saw a bumper sticker that said it this way: "All I want is a little more than I have now."

We often think that things or events can make us happy, and they often do—for a while. But they can never bring *lasting* happiness. You can be truly happy, though, when you discover where happiness begins. Try putting Jesus first in your life. Obey Him and help other people, thinking more of their needs than your own. You will discover that Jesus alone is the Source of as much happiness and joy as you can possibly hold.

ENJOYING GOD'S PRESENCE

In Your presence is fullness of joy.
PSALM 16:11

When a bride walks down the aisle on her father's arm, everyone at the wedding is looking at her. But she and her groom, who's waiting at the front of the church, are looking only at each other. Their smiles and their sparkling eyes say, "I love you!" They are filled with joy at being with the one they love.

Even though we can't see God, He is with us, and being with Him brings us great joy. We feel it when we listen to Him speak in His Word, when we read the Bible, and when we pray. But it also happens as we simply enjoy knowing God—as we think about His goodness, delight in the beautiful world He created, or rejoice in the surprise of an unexpected blessing.

The Bible says, "Be still, and know that I am God" (Psalm 46:10). Someday we will be with God forever. But in the meantime, enjoy His love and goodness now, for He is with you every hour of the day.

HEAVEN, THE HAPPIEST PLACE

You have a better and an enduring possession for yourselves in heaven.
HEBREWS 10:34

Where is the happiest place on earth? It is somewhere you feel happy and understood and loved. It might be in your home, or with your friends, or even at Disneyland. But do you know where the happiest place *not* on earth is? If you said "Heaven," you were right.

Some people think Heaven will be dull and boring, but that's not true! Jesus Himself will be there! And our home in Heaven will be a happy home because there will be joyful work to do. The apostle John wrote in Revelation 22:3, "His servants shall serve Him." This means we will be given exactly the tasks that fit our interests and abilities. It will be a great privilege to serve Jesus in His heavenly home!

Have you ever been to a new school or church and felt lonely or strange? Then if you saw a familiar face, didn't you feel so much better? In Heaven we will never feel lonely or strange, because we will be surrounded by our friends and family, the family of God. Heaven is the place where we will be most loved.

GOD IS WITH US

"I am with you always, to the very end of the age."
MATTHEW 28:20 NIV

If your house catches fire or someone needs an ambulance, what do you do? You call 911! Almost anywhere in the United States and Canada, calling 911 connects you to an emergency dispatch center. The dispatcher sees where the call is coming from and sends help to that location right away—day or night.

Jesus' promise "I am with you always" is a little bit like our 911 system. The word *always* in that promise means "all the days, all day long." We can count on Jesus being with us not only every day but every moment of every day, and every night! When we need help, He is already there.

Psalm 77:1 says, "I call to God, and he will hear me" (ICB). We just need to realize He is with us—as close as a whisper and a prayer. This happens as we speak to Him when we worship and pray and listen to Him speak to us through His Word, the Bible. Call out to God, and you will see what it feels like to be loved by the One who loves you perfectly and will always, always be with you.

THE TUG OF GOD'S LOVE

The Spirit Himself bears witness with our spirit that we are children of God.
ROMANS 8:16

Whenever anyone asks me how I can be so certain who God is and what He is like, I think about this story. On a windy day with big puffy clouds, a boy went out to fly his kite. The kite went up and up and up until it was hidden by the clouds.

"What are you doing?" a man asked the boy.

"I'm flying a kite," the boy replied.

"Flying a kite?" asked the man. "How can you be sure? You can't see the kite."

"No," said the boy, "I can't see it, but I can feel it tug, so I know for sure it's there!"

God is real. Don't let anyone fool you into believing that He's not. His presence is just as sure as the tug on a young boy's kite. And His love is just like the wind that carries the kite high into the sky. You can't see the wind, but you know for sure it is there.

God is real. His love is real. Find out for yourself by inviting Jesus to come into your life to forgive your sins. Then you will know by the wonderful, warm tug on your heart that He is there for sure.

THE BEST REST

"Come to Me, all you who labor and are heavy
laden, and I will give you rest."
MATTHEW 11:28

God designed some animals to hibernate to survive winter's cold temperatures and scarce food sources. When a bat or a wood frog hibernates, it goes into a deep sleep. Its breathing slows or even stops. It doesn't eat or drink. Other animals, like ground squirrels and bears, hibernate more lightly and do wake up to eat from time to time. When spring comes, hibernating animals get up, ready for active days once again.

People don't hibernate, but we do need rest. We need good sleep at night. Sometimes we need a break from our busy schedules. Sometimes people say they need a vacation just to rest from their vacation! Perhaps we have been looking for rest in the wrong places.

Jesus said, "Come to Me . . . and I will give you rest." Jesus gives us the best rest. With Jesus, we don't have to worry about the future. So rest in Him, and don't worry about what lies ahead. Jesus has already taken care of tomorrow!

STAY FILLED UP

Be filled with the Spirit.
EPHESIANS 5:18 NIV

When the logs in a campfire have been burned up, the fire goes out. When a car has traveled many miles and the gas tank is empty, the car won't run. If power lines snap during a storm, the lights go out. But finding more logs, stopping to refuel, and calling the power company will eventually get everything going again.

You might think that the Holy Spirit works in our lives the same way. But God's supply of the Spirit never runs out! The command "Be filled with the Spirit" actually has the idea of being filled continuously, or all the time, never running out! This verse could say, "Be filled and keep on being filled."

The Bible says, "God has poured out his love to fill our hearts. God gave us his love through the Holy Spirit" (Romans 5:5 ICB). The Holy Spirit should flow in us and through us all the time—and He will, as we follow and obey Jesus every day.

CHILDREN OF LIGHT

You are all children of the light.
1 THESSALONIANS 5:5 NLT

Being in the dark can be a little scary sometimes. You can't see where you are, what's around you, or where you're going. But once you turn on a light, you can see everything clearly again.

There's another kind of darkness called *spiritual blindness*. That means we can't see clearly what is true. Jesus said He came to preach "recovery of sight to the blind" (Luke 4:18). Because of sin, we can't see spiritual truth clearly. But the Spirit of God helps us see our sin and our helplessness and shows us God's saving gift of Jesus. The Spirit shows us the truth of Jesus' words, "I am the light of the world. He who follows Me shall not walk in darkness, but have the light of life" (John 8:12).

In the Bible we are called "children of light and children of the day" (1 Thessalonians 5:5 NRSV). We are no longer in the dark—we know where we came from, we know why we are here, and we know where we are going. Be sure to live as a child of the light each day!

LIFE FOREVER

For to me, to live is Christ, and to die is gain.
PHILIPPIANS 1:21

Scientific experiments and explorations look for evidence to explain how the world works—things like gravity, the water cycle, and why seasons change. But I have asked a number of scientists questions about life after death, and most of them say, "We just do not know." Scientists can't *observe* eternal life, so they can't explain it.

During the forty days after Jesus' resurrection, many people saw Jesus. On one occasion, as many as five hundred people saw Him at one time. They knew He had died. They saw Him alive again!

Jesus said, "I am the resurrection and the life. He who believes in Me, though he may die, he shall live. And whoever lives and believes in Me shall never die" (John 11:25–26). Our hope of eternal life is based on Jesus alone. Because we know He is alive, we have hope—hope for today and for life that never ends.

BECAUSE OF PRAYER

The effective, fervent prayer of a righteous man avails much.

JAMES 5:16

In a Nazi prison camp during World War II, Corrie ten Boom saw and experienced much cruelty from prison guards. Corrie's sister, Betsie, and many others died there. When Corrie was released at the end of the war, she faced a challenge. She knew she should forgive those who treated her so badly, but she didn't want to. What would she do?

Corrie prayed about it. God's love filled her heart, and she was able to forgive. For the rest of her life, Corrie told her story and taught and inspired many people to forgive others too.

Lives change when people pray. History has been changed time after time because of prayer, and history can be changed again when we pray, ask for God's will to be done, and believe God will answer. Pray today for neighbors and kids at school who don't know Jesus yet. God still works through the prayers of His people!

JANUARY 25

TURN TROUBLE INTO JOY

Whenever you face trials of any kind, consider it nothing but joy.
JAMES 1:2 NRSV

When she got the news that she had cancer, Lauren Hill was looking forward to playing college basketball. Lauren's cancer was a type of brain tumor that usually affects younger children and has no cure. Lauren could have chosen to feel sorry for herself and become sad and bitter—but she didn't. Instead, she used her situation to raise awareness of her disease and to raise money to help find a cure for other children in the future.

Her debut college game was moved up a few weeks, and more than ten thousand people came. Lauren played in that game for a short time, and forty thousand dollars was donated for cancer research that day. "Even though I'm probably not going to be around to see it, it's going to help a lot of people," Lauren said. When she died on April 10, 2015, Lauren had raised more than $1.5 million to help the search for a cure.

Yes, it's hard to "consider it nothing but joy" when difficult problems come. But when they do, ask God to bless and use those difficulties to make you strong in your faith and to help others.

TALKING TO GOD

Oh that men would praise the LORD for his goodness, and
for his wonderful works to the children of men!

PSALM 107:8 KJV

When you were very young and learning to talk, did you speak to your parents in long sentences for hours at a time? I doubt it. And yet your parents weren't disappointed in you; they were delighted by your first attempts to speak.

In the same way, when we truly understand that God is our loving heavenly Father and we are His children, we never need to worry about disappointing Him with our prayers. No matter how short or simple our words, if our prayers express our true feelings and desires, God delights in them.

Here is a pattern to help you learn to pray. Begin by thanking God for all He has done for you and praising Him for His love and goodness. Then confess your sins and ask for His forgiveness. Finally, bring your concerns to Him. You may even find it helpful to keep a list of people you are praying for.

Remember: Jesus Christ opened Heaven's door for us by His death on the cross. When we know Him, we can be sure God hears our prayers.

ABOVE THE NOISE

Let this mind be in you which was also in Christ Jesus.
PHILIPPIANS 2:5

Airplanes can be noisy places. The air going through the big jet engines makes noise. The air rushing over and around the body of the plane makes noise. And the movable parts of the plane, like the wing flaps and landing gear, also make noise. Passengers can wear noise-canceling headphones to block all that noise *and* hear only the music they want to listen to or the movie they want to watch.

All around us, the world makes a lot of noise too. In music videos, TV shows, movies, and social media, the world calls out for us to put money, fun, and possessions ahead of God in our lives.

But for Christians, the Bible is like noise-canceling headphones. God's Word cancels out the noise of the world and lets us hear what God says is true. Romans 12:2 says, "Do not be shaped by this world. Instead be changed within by a new way of thinking. Then you will be able to decide what God wants for you. And you will be able to know what is good and pleasing to God and what is perfect" (ICB).

Spend time with the Bible every day. Don't let the world shape your mind. Let God do it!

WHAT–IF WORRIES

Let your requests be made known to God; and the peace
of God . . . will guard your hearts and minds.
PHILIPPIANS 4:6–7

Mark Twain, author of *The Adventures of Tom Sawyer* and *The Adventures of Huckleberry Finn*, is believed to have said, "I've had a lot of worries in my life, most of which never happened."

Do you worry about things that might happen? *What if my friend moves away? What if I get a bad grade? What if my mom loses her job? What if I don't make the team?* No problems upset us as much as what-if worries—troubles that haven't happened yet and might never happen. Worrying about what might happen makes even the smallest trouble seem huge. For example, if you spend all your time worrying about an upcoming test, you won't have any time to study for it!

Instead of worrying so much, listen instead to Jesus' promise: "Peace I leave with you, My peace I give to you; not as the world gives do I give to you. Let not your heart be troubled, neither let it be afraid" (John 14:27).

Is something worrying you right now? Give it to Jesus, and trust Him to take care of it or to show you what to do. Let His peace take the place of all your worries.

A SPECIAL INVITATION

"My Father will honor anyone who serves me."
JOHN 12:26 ICB

Each year Operation Christmas Child delivers gift-filled shoeboxes to children in need around the world to demonstrate God's love for them. The project began with just two people in Wales who wanted to help orphans in Romania. Now families, churches, and other groups in many different countries fill shoeboxes with gifts for millions of children each year. And along with toys, school supplies, and hygiene items, the shoeboxes contain a storybook with the gospel and an invitation to learn more about Jesus.

Children like you often are involved in selecting and packing items for these shoeboxes. Young people want adventure and excitement, but also a cause to believe in. The only cause big enough to satisfy the longing of our hearts is the cause of Jesus Christ, and the invitation to be Jesus' disciples is the most thrilling invitation we could ever imagine. Think of it—the God of the universe invites us to become His partners in loving and saving the world for Him! We can each have a part, using the special gifts and opportunities God has given us.

Christ's call is for us to be His disciples every day. How are you responding to His call?

LIVING STONES

You also, as living stones, are being built up a spiritual house.
1 PETER 2:5

I have a friend who lost his job, his savings, and his home, and then his wife died. But he held on tight to his faith in Christ—the only thing he had left. Like Job in the Old Testament, he would not give up on God, no matter what happened. Also just like Job, however, he wondered *why* these things had happened to him.

One day he saw some men doing stonework on a huge church. One of them was chiseling a small piece of stone into a triangle.

"What are you going to do with that?" my friend asked.

"See that little opening way up there near the top?" the workman replied. "Well, I'm shaping this down here so it will fit in perfectly up there."

Tears filled my friend's eyes as he walked away. It seemed that God had spoken through the workman to explain the hard times he was going through: "I'm shaping you down here so you'll fit in up there."

WHAT'S YOUR OS?

Be changed within by a new way of thinking.
ROMANS 12:2 ICB

A computer needs an operating system, or OS, to manage its hardware, memory, processes, and any other software it is running. The operating system controls what the computer can do, and if the OS gets a virus or a worm or some other problem, the computer won't work right at all.

The Bible teaches that we need Jesus to be the operating system of our minds, because how we think determines what we do. God wants to change us to be like Jesus, so first He changes our thinking as we fill up our minds with His Word. And He tells us to keep our minds working the way they should by keeping the wrong things out. This is why we are careful about the music we listen to, the movies and TV we watch, the books we read, and the things we think about.

Keep your operating system working right today. Ask God to help you fill your mind with thoughts shaped by His Word.

FEBRUARY

Your faithfulness reaches to the clouds.

PSALM 36:5

WHAT TO DO TODAY

Work as if you were working for the Lord.
COLOSSIANS 3:23 ICB

Have you ever built a sand castle at the beach? Did you know that there are sand-sculpting contests all over the world? Some people actually get paid to create sand sculptures for others to enjoy. But no matter which sand creation wins a contest or how big it is, eventually it will crumble. Nothing made of sand can last.

Someone once wrote, "Only one life, 'twill soon be past; only what's done for Christ will last." Every day we live is a new opportunity to love and please God. We will never live *this* day again—once it is gone, it's gone forever. How will you spend today? Will you try to be loving, like God is, and show others His goodness? Will you be living for yourself or for God? Remember, "Only what's done for Christ will last."

ALWAYS WITH US

No good thing will He withhold from those who walk uprightly.

PSALM 84:11

What have been some of your happiest times? Christmas or your birthday? Sledding or riding a roller coaster? Winning a big game for your team?

Jesus wants to be part of every experience and every moment of our lives—the hard times *and* the happy times! During Jesus' time on earth, He visited friends at their homes, joined the fun at parties, and held babies and blessed children. Sometimes the examples in His stories made people laugh, like the one about a camel trying to go through the eye of a needle.

Someone has said, "There are just as many stars in the sky at noon as there are at midnight. We just can't see them when the sun is shining." Just as those stars are there when we can't see them, God is with us when we have problems. He helps us and takes care of us in ways we sometimes don't even understand. And because He loves us so much, He's right there with us in all our good times too! So let's thank Him for our happy times and for being with us always.

FEBRUARY 3

ABOVE THE CLOUDS

Your faithfulness reaches to the clouds.
PSALM 36:5

My home is on a mountain nearly four thousand feet high. Often I can look down and see clouds in the valley below. Some mornings I wake up to sunshine, but the valley is covered with clouds. Other times, storms blow into the valley, and I can see lightning flash and hear thunder roar below me while I enjoy sunlight and blue sky above the storm.

Many times as I sit on my front porch, I think about how the discouragement we feel and troubles we go through are like those clouds. They can seem to hide the sunlight of God's love from us for a while. But just as the sky is bright above the storm clouds, He is still there!

God doesn't just walk away from His children. We can always put our faith in Him and trust His promise: "I will never leave you nor forsake you" (Hebrews 13:5).

LOVE IN ACTION

He loved us and sent his Son as a sacrifice to take away our sins.

1 JOHN 4:10 NLT

We use the word *love* to mean many different kinds of feelings. We say we love doing gymnastics or eating peanut butter and jelly sandwiches. We love our favorite holidays, video games, and TV shows too. But "loving" those things is different from loving our parents, grandparents, brothers, sisters, and friends. And it is different from God's love for us, which is the greatest love of all.

The Bible says, "But God demonstrates His own love toward us, in that while we were still sinners, Christ died for us" (Romans 5:8). Even before He created the world, God planned to send Jesus. He knew we would need a Savior.

God shows His love for us with action. Now that is real love!

LONGING FOR GOD

My whole being wants to be with the living God.
PSALM 84:2 ICB

Have you ever dived into a swimming pool to pick up something from the bottom—maybe a large ring or coin? Before long, whether or not you found what you were looking for, you had to come back to the surface to get a breath. You might have even rushed to the top because you really needed to breathe!

Longing for God can feel like that too. We feel empty and know that we need Him, even more than we need air.

Nothing will ever satisfy us more than God Himself, and when we know Him well, we have everything we need. King David wrote, "Surely your goodness and love will be with me all my life" (Psalm 23:6 ICB). So go ahead—dive in! Today, read about God's love for you in Psalm 23, and thank Him for the good things He brings.

UNTIL JESUS COMES

> The day the Lord comes again will be a surprise
> like a thief that comes in the night.
> 1 THESSALONIANS 5:2 ICB

Sometimes you hear bad news that worries you—a huge storm that destroys homes or a war in another country. Sometimes the bad news is closer—there's a bully or someone who makes fun of Christians at your school.

The Bible says that in all these situations, we need to comfort one another with the reminder that one day Jesus is coming back to make everything right! We don't know when this will be, but it *will* happen!

Many times when I go to bed at night, I think that before I wake up, Jesus could come. Sometimes when I get up and look at the sunrise, I think, *Perhaps this is the day He will return.*

But until that day, God is still working—and so should we. No matter what's going on, we need to pray, and we need to do what we can to help others and show them Jesus' love. After all, Jesus tells His people, "Let your light so shine before men, that they may see your good works and glorify your Father in heaven" (Matthew 5:16).

THE BREAD OF LIFE

He who wins souls is wise.
PROVERBS 11:30

Thomas Edison was an inventor who figured out how to make the kind of light bulbs people can use in their homes. Edison tried six thousand different materials before he found one that worked! If he had given up before he found the right material, he wouldn't have been able to give electric light to the world.

Christians have bread and water for the world. The Bible calls Jesus "the Bread of Life" and "the Living Water" (John 4:10; 6:35). People may be so busy filling up on other things that they ignore Him or turn away from us when we point them to Him, but we need to keep inviting them to come to Jesus. Sometimes they can't come, and we have to carry the Bread and Water to them.

We must keep on and not give up. Jesus never gave up on His mission, and we are His followers. All around you are people who hunger and thirst for God, but they may not even realize it. Will you point them to Jesus? He's the only One who can satisfy their hunger and thirst.

BEHIND US

You have cast all my sins behind Your back.

ISAIAH 38:17

One morning when I was crossing the Atlantic Ocean on a ship, I looked out my window as I got up and saw one of the blackest clouds ever! I was sure we were in for a terrible storm. When I ordered my breakfast, I spoke to the waiter about it. He said, "Oh, we've already come through that storm. It's behind us!"

How do you feel when something difficult is behind you, like when your piano recital is over, or you finish a test in your hardest subject? You probably feel relieved and say, "I'm so glad that's over!"

If we believe in Jesus, we can be glad every day that something else very difficult—God's judgment of our sins—is behind us. It happened at the cross! The penalty for our sins has already been paid by Christ, completely and fully. That's how much God loves us!

THE MEANING OF THE CROSS

You are my hope, O Lord God; You are my trust from my youth.
PSALM 71:5

To people coming from other countries to live in the United States, the Statue of Liberty is a symbol—a sign—of freedom and opportunity. It's like the way the colors of a traffic light are symbols for *stop*, *go*, and *slow down*, or a heart shape is a symbol of love. All symbols have meaning. The cross is a symbol with many meanings.

First, it reminds us of Jesus' death. The cross tells us that Jesus closed the gap between God and us. Second, the cross tells us who we truly are: forgiven sinners who now belong to God. The cross symbolizes our eternal destiny and our true purpose: to love God and serve Him with all our might.

People can be confused about the answers to big questions like, "Where did we come from?" "Why are we here?" and "Where are we going?" The cross is a symbol of hope in the darkness and doubt. It leads us to the right answers!

The next time you see a cross, stop to think about what Jesus did on the cross and what difference it makes in your life.

GROWING BY OBEYING

The Lord our God we will serve, and His voice we will obey!
JOSHUA 24:24

I knew a father who refused to get his son a bicycle even though he had money to buy it. He wasn't being cruel or stingy; he simply knew his son needed to learn responsibility before he owned a bike. The boy often forgot his chores or refused to do his homework.

Just like that father, God wants His children to learn responsibility. Yes, we are saved by His grace—but we are also called to become dependable disciples.

We learn to follow Jesus by obeying God's Word. In the Old Testament, the prophet Samuel warned the Israelites, "If you do not obey the voice of the Lord, but rebel against the commandment of the Lord, then the hand of the Lord will be against you" (1 Samuel 12:15).

You might not know everything God wants you to do right now, but you do know some things . . . so do those things! As you learn more, you'll be able to do more. God is good, and He knows it takes time to learn to be dependable disciples. Keep obeying His Word. He'll help you grow in wonderful ways!

FEBRUARY 11

NOT FAITH BUT SIGHT

"The Son of Man will come in the glory of His Father with His angels."
MATTHEW 16:27

Have you ever read a book or watched a movie that was so good you didn't stop to eat or do your homework or your chores? The characters and events seemed so real that for a little while you forgot where you were and what you were supposed to be doing!

We can't see Jesus today (although through the Holy Spirit, He lives in our hearts). But someday in the future, we will "see Him as He is" (1 John 3:2). Everyone will see Jesus when He comes again! He will come with His angels and defeat every enemy, and we will live with Him forever.

But just like it's easy to get "lost" in a good book or movie, it's easy to get so involved in our everyday lives that we forget all about the promise of eternity! The present seems so real, and the unseen future seems so unreal, but actually the opposite is true. So don't give all your attention to your present circumstances. Instead, "seek those things which are above, where Christ is" (Colossians 3:1).

WAITING ON GOD

But those who wait on the LORD shall renew their strength;
they shall mount up with wings like eagles.
ISAIAH 40:31

Eagles are large and strong carnivores—which means they hunt and eat meat—and they have especially sharp eyesight. They also have the unusual ability to lock their joints and soar in the wind instead of flapping their wings. All around the world, and in the Bible, the eagle is a symbol of power.

The Bible tells us we can face trouble with a power others do not have—the power of God. Christians may have problems and experience sickness and disasters, like floods and tornadoes, just as other people do. But as we trust Him, God helps us go through suffering and see something good come out of it.

As we wait on God, He helps us use the winds of trouble to soar above our problems like an eagle soars through the air. As the Bible says, "Those who wait on the LORD . . . shall mount up with wings like eagles."

FEBRUARY 13

A JOYFUL LIFE

Rejoice in the Lord always.
PHILIPPIANS 4:4

How many times did you smile today? Some people say we use more muscles when we frown than when we smile, but the truth is that frowns and smiles use about the same number. So why not smile instead of frown? It'll make us—and people around us—feel happier!

The Christian life is a happy, joyful life. Christianity was never meant to make people miserable. Jesus served other people with joy. The Bible tells us that peace and victory over sin are ours. This is good news that should make us smile!

When we want the will of God for our lives, then we are happy for God to use us any way He pleases. Our plans and desires begin to agree with His, and we accept His direction in our lives. We feel more joy and peace, no matter what our situation, if we are doing what God wants.

"What a witness to the world Christians would be," wrote Amy Carmichael, a missionary and author, "if only they were more evidently very happy people." Joy is one of the marks of a believer. Will others see the joy of Jesus in your life today?

FOLLOWING JESUS AT HOME

"I am the vine, you are the branches. He who abides
in Me, and I in him, bears much fruit."
JOHN 15:5

We can look good, for a while at least, if we're trying hard to fit in with people who don't know us well. But how we act when we *aren't* trying to impress anyone is the real test for Christians. How do we act around the people who know us best—our families?

They see us as we really are. They see us when we're tired, stressed, worried, and angry. They know whether Jesus lives in and through us.

Someone who is truly following Jesus will not often give in at home to anger, impatience, criticizing, sarcasm, unkindness, suspicion, selfishness, or laziness. Instead, that person's life will display the fruit of the Spirit: "love, joy, peace, patience, kindness, goodness, faithfulness, gentleness and self-control" (Galatians 5:22–23 NIV).

How do you act at home? What does your behavior at home tell people about you?

FEBRUARY 15

TURN THE WORLD UPSIDE DOWN

They were all filled with the Holy Spirit.
ACTS 2:4

The early Christians had no church buildings, no TV or Internet, no airplanes or cars, no phones or books. Yet they turned their world "upside down" for Jesus (Acts 17:6). When they began to share the gospel and live for Jesus, life as everyone knew it began to change.

Even though many of them lost their jobs or were forced out of town, the early Christians stayed courageous, bold, and full of faith. They lived their lives daily for Christ, no matter what others thought, preaching the gospel and doing good for others. Some even died for their faith in Christ.

What was the secret of how these early Christians lived? The Bible tells us: "They were all filled with the Holy Spirit." The Holy Spirit changed their lives, and then the people around them couldn't help but notice their love and good lives. What keeps us from turning our world upside down for Christ?

SERVING GOD FOREVER

Because of His great love . . . He . . . made us alive together with Christ.
EPHESIANS 2:4–5

D o you ever get bored? You may have school and sports and church activities, but perhaps life doesn't seem very exciting sometimes. Did you know that in Heaven we will never grow bored?

I've heard some people who don't believe in Jesus doubt that Heaven is real. Once a man said to me, "You might be mistaken about Heaven. No one has ever come back from the dead to tell us for sure."

"Sir, that's exactly where you are wrong," I replied. "Someone has returned—His name is Jesus Christ, our Lord."

That makes all the difference! Jesus is alive, and we know there are blessings kept for us in Heaven. "They cannot be destroyed or be spoiled or lose their beauty" (1 Peter 1:4 ICB). Heaven is an amazing place in the presence of God, which guarantees you'll never be bored there!

POWER FOR LIFE

"The Spirit of truth . . . dwells with you and will be in you."
JOHN 14:17

A young girl asked her father, an electrician, "Daddy, how can I believe in the Holy Spirit when I have never seen Him?"

"I'll show you how," said her father. He took his daughter to a power plant and showed her the generators. "This is where electric power comes from," he said. "We can't see the power, but it's in those machines and in the power lines, and then it heats our stove and gives us light.

"Do you believe in electricity?" the dad asked.

"Yes, I believe in electricity," said the girl.

"Of course you do," said her father, "but you don't believe in it because you see it. You believe in it because you see what it can do. That's the same reason you can believe in the Holy Spirit. Not because you see Him, but because you see what He does in people's lives when they are following Jesus and filled with His power."

Look around you—can you see the Holy Spirit at work? If someone trusts in Jesus and is being kind and loving, if someone says, "I forgive you" or "God is good, and I trust Him" . . . then the answer is yes!

GOD TAKES THE BURDEN

As a father has compassion on his children, so the
LORD has compassion on those who fear him.
PSALM 103:13 NIV

Children aren't expected to have jobs and earn money for food, clothing, and a place to live. They assume—and they have a right to—that their parents will provide everything they need. Parents are responsible for taking care of their children.

We are God's children. Jesus said, "Do not worry, saying, 'What shall we eat?' or 'What shall we drink?' or 'What shall we wear?' . . . But seek first the kingdom of God . . . and all these things shall be added to you" (Matthew 6:31, 33). Because we are God's children, He tells us that He is responsible for taking care of us.

Unfortunately, worry is a habit for most of us. But the Bible tells us to give all our worries to Him, because He cares for us (1 Peter 5:7). In other words, let God do the worrying! He says, "I'll take the burden. Don't give it a thought—leave it to Me."

Never forget: God is bigger than your problems. Whatever worries you might have today, put them in God's hands—and leave them there.

FEBRUARY 19

GOD'S PEACE PLAN

Great peace have those who love Your law, and
nothing causes them to stumble.
PSALM 119:165

When a war ends, the countries that have been fighting sign a *treaty*. It's an agreement to stop fighting and live in peace.

God has a plan for peace, and it's found in His Son, Jesus, who the Bible calls the "Prince of Peace" (Isaiah 9:6). Why? Because Jesus said the problem is within us: "All these evil things begin inside a person, in the mind: evil thoughts, . . . stealing, murder, . . . selfishness, doing bad things to other people, lying, doing sinful things, jealousy, saying bad things about people, pride, and foolish living" (Mark 7:21–22 ICB). What a list!

Our sin is like a fight against God, but God longs for us to have peace. That's why Jesus came. His death for our sins is God's peace treaty—it's the way for us to have peace with God! As we repent and receive Jesus, the war is over, for God extends a peace treaty to all who come to Him.

A WARNING LIGHT

My child, if you are wise, then I will be happy.

PROVERBS 23:15 ICB

The bright light shining out from a lighthouse helps ships navigate at night and warns them of dangers in the water. God has given us all something like that called our *conscience*. It helps us know what's good and bad and guides us away from danger.

The conscience has been called "the light of the soul." Have you ever felt a "warning light" go on inside you when you thought about doing something wrong? That's your conscience. God uses it to steer you away from evil and toward good. The Bible says, "The Lord looks into a person's feelings. He searches through a person's thoughts" (Proverbs 20:27 ICB). He knows right where you are and wants to help you choose what's best.

Our conscience can be our gentlest teacher and friend. But continuing to sin can dull or even silence our conscience. On the other hand, paying attention to God's Word will sharpen our conscience and make us more sensitive to what is right and wrong.

ANYWHERE, ANYTIME

Always be joyful. Never stop praying.
1 THESSALONIANS 5:16–17 NLT

If we go too long without the right foods, our bodies don't get the vitamins and minerals they need to be strong and healthy. In the same way, if we go too long without praying, we can't be spiritually strong and healthy. In fact, the Bible says, "Pray continually"—without stopping (1 Thessalonians 5:17 NIV). But we have lots of other things to do every day. How do we pray continually?

It isn't enough to get out of bed in the morning, quickly bow our heads, and repeat a few sentences. Instead, we need to set aside time to be alone with God, speaking to Him in prayer and listening to Him speak through His Word. If you set aside special times for prayer, your mind will be filled with those prayers all day long even when you aren't thinking about them.

The second way to pray continually is to realize that we can pray in our hearts and minds anywhere, anytime—and God will hear us! You can pray silently while you are riding your bike, studying for a test, or making an important decision. Today let prayer fill your life all day long!

MAKE ROOM

Commit your way to the LORD . . . and He shall bring it to pass.
PSALM 37:5

Have you ever planted a garden? Maybe you planted carrots and zucchini, or maybe you planted flowers. One thing's for sure—your garden also grew some weeds! And if you didn't pull the weeds out, soon there wasn't any room for vegetables or flowers to grow.

Just like a garden has room for only healthy plants *or* weeds, but not both, two opposite forces can't exist in one human heart at the same time. If there's lots of doubt, faith can't last. If there's hatred or selfishness, love gets crowded out. If we're filled with worry, there's no room for trust.

And in the same way, God won't share His place in our lives with anything or anyone less than Himself. Is anything crowding God out of your heart today? Don't let that happen. Instead, "commit your way to the LORD."

FEBRUARY 23

LET IT SHINE!

The light of the righteous rejoices.
PROVERBS 13:9

Some things start out small but turn out big. A tall, sturdy oak tree grows from a tiny acorn. A little flame can turn into a huge campfire. A simple smile at someone new can begin a lasting friendship.

The gospel is like that too. Sometimes the world seems cold and unfriendly, and we wonder how the simple salvation message of Jesus can make an impact. But it always does. Even a small light breaks through darkness. Someone will be warmed by the fire of God's love.

So keep on shining the light God's given you—the light of His love and truth—even when your light seems small. Remember that "with God all things are possible" (Matthew 19:26), and He will bless your efforts to bring the good news of Jesus to the world!

IT'S FREE!

"Come, buy . . . without money and without price."
ISAIAH 55:1

A Sunday school teacher stood in front of each of her students and held out a dollar bill. "I have a gift for you," she said. The students who took the bill got to keep it as a gift. Students who didn't reach out to take the dollar didn't get the gift. It didn't take long for everyone in the room to understand the lesson: God holds our salvation in His hand, and He offers it as a free gift, "without money and without price." We just have to reach out and accept the gift.

But something as precious as salvation must cost us greatly, we think. *Doesn't God want us to work hard to earn our salvation?*

No. And the reason is that the price has already been paid. Salvation is free—but it wasn't cheap. It cost the dear Son of God His very life.

The best things in life are free—the air we breathe, the stars at night, the love we share with family. But the greatest gift of all is our salvation, purchased for us by Jesus Christ. "Thanks be to God for His indescribable gift!" (2 Corinthians 9:15).

IN THE FIRE

"You shall receive power when the Holy Spirit has come
upon you; and you shall be witnesses to Me."
ACTS 1:8

Can you guess what happens when sand is mixed with some chemicals and heated to over two thousand degrees for several hours? The combination becomes melted glass. When it melts, the glass becomes soft enough that someone can shape it into figures or jewelry. The transformation from start to finish is amazing!

Did you know God transforms us in amazing ways too? Before the crucifixion, the disciple Peter bragged that he would never deny Jesus, and then *three times* Peter ended up telling people he didn't even know Him. But after Peter was transformed by God's love and the Holy Spirit, he boldly and fearlessly proclaimed the good news of salvation (Acts 2:36). Peter the weak was transformed into Peter the rock.

The Holy Spirit changed all the early disciples. Their faith and zeal started a "fire of faith" that spread throughout the Roman Empire. They were completely submitted to Jesus and His will. Today, ask God to transform you into someone who can boldly tell others about God's love!

GIVING BACK

No good thing will He withhold from those who walk uprightly.

PSALM 84:11

It's easy to take our blessings for granted and not think about them very much. Our safety and health, our freedom, our five senses, our family's love, the fact that we're alive—these are all blessings from the hand of God. Most of all, God has given us the gift of salvation through Jesus.

What should our response be? One word: *thankfulness*. But how do we show our thankfulness? We say thank you to God by giving back to Him a part of what He has given us.

Once a boy in a crowd listening to Jesus gave up his lunch of five little loaves of bread and two small fish. Everyone in the crowd was hungry, and only the boy had any food. Jesus used the boy's gift to feed more than five thousand hungry people!

Are you thankful for your blessings? What could you do to show your thanks to God for all He has done, and is doing, for you?

A PERMANENT PLACE

"In My Father's house are many mansions."
JOHN 14:2

Have you ever gone camping? It's fun to set up tents and stow your gear inside. You cook and eat and wash dishes outdoors, even at night. For a while, your campsite is your home.

But campsites aren't permanent places to live. Eventually it's time to break camp. And when you get back home, well, that feels good too! There's just no place like home.

The disciples who gave up their houses and lands to follow Jesus and tell others about Him didn't get to enjoy having a home—a place of comfort to share with people they loved. It was as if Jesus was saying to them, "We have no lasting home here on earth, but my Father's house is a home where we will be together for all eternity."

Even life's happiest experiences last only a short time, but the joy we'll know in Heaven will be permanent. Someday we will get to go to that wonderful, happy home! Jesus will be there to welcome us, and we will never have to leave!

PLEASING GOD

I have learned how to be content with whatever I have.

PHILIPPIANS 4:11 NLT

Dogs have been called "man's best friend." When a dog knows it is loved, it loves back. Dogs *want* to please their owners.

People, on the other hand, have to *decide* who they want to please. Do you want the popular kids at school to think you're cool? Do you want praise for your soccer skills? Or do you just want to do your best and please God with your actions every day?

Popularity and praise feel good, but they can be dangerous too. They can turn us away from God without us even realizing it, making us like those in Jesus' day who "loved the praise of men more than the praise of God" (John 12:43).

Ask God to keep you from worrying about what others think and to help you be content with whatever He sends your way. All the tomorrows of your life have to pass by Him before they get to you! The important thing is to have one goal—to please Christ—and to remember that whatever happens, He is with us.

MARCH

"'Love the LORD your God with all your heart' . . .
and 'your neighbor as yourself.'"
LUKE 10:27

MARCH 1

IN THE WORLD, NOT OF THE WORLD

They are of the world. . . . We are of God.
1 JOHN 4:5—6

A strong current of warm water called the Gulf Stream flows through the ocean, but doesn't mix with it! The Gulf Stream stays at a warm temperature, even in the icy waters of the North Atlantic Ocean. The Gulf Stream is *in* the ocean, but doesn't act like part of it.

Believers are *in* the world, but not part of it. We should never be pulled into the wrong thinking and activities of our friends who don't know God. The Bible says, "Do not be shaped by this world" (Romans 12:2 ICB). Jesus spent time with people the religious leaders called sinners. In fact, they called Jesus a Friend of sinners. But Jesus didn't let those friends change Him. Instead, He used every opportunity to share God's truth and help people come to know God.

You can have many different friends, but always look for opportunities to share your faith with those who don't know Jesus yet. Like the warm Gulf Stream, can you be around people who may not be following Jesus and yet not act like them? Will the friends you spend time with today see the love and goodness of Jesus in you?

PEOPLE OF PRAYER

Lord, teach us to pray.
LUKE 11:1

Some people pray only when they are stressed out or in danger. It is good for us to pray in times of trouble. In those moments we realize our helplessness and that only God can change things. But we shouldn't *only* pray in times of trouble or when we need something. There are many other times to pray too! We can thank God for a new day when we wake up and ask Him to watch over us as we sleep. In between, we can thank Him for the fun we had with our friends, talk to Him about someone who is sick, or even ask for help in understanding our math or reading homework. God loves to hear from us anytime!

Jesus prayed alone and with His friends. Once, after He finished praying, His followers said, "Lord, teach us to pray." They wanted to be in touch with God the way Jesus was.

Have you ever said, "Lord, teach me to pray"? Prayer can be as much a part of our lives as breathing. Our world needs people who pray. Will you be one of them?

WE CAN COUNT ON GOD

Blessed is the man whose strength is in You.
PSALM 84:5

Someone wrote a little verse that goes:

> Said the robin to the sparrow,
> "I should really like to know,
> Why these anxious human beings
> Rush about and worry so."
> Said the sparrow to the robin,
> "Friend, I think that it must be,
> That they have no heavenly Father
> Such as cares for you and me."

Jesus used the no-worry attitude of birds as an example in His teaching: "Look at the birds of the air, for they neither sow nor reap . . . yet your heavenly Father feeds them" (Matthew 6:26). If God cares for hungry birds and fragile flowers in such wonderful ways, we can count on Him for every aspect of our lives. After all, He loves us so much, He sent His Son into the world to save us. That's how valuable we are to Him!

LOVE YOUR NEIGHBOR

The whole law is made complete in this one command:
"Love your neighbor as you love yourself."

GALATIANS 5:14 ICB

Try to think of a time when you made a point to help someone—maybe you helped clean up a mess you didn't make, or you gave some of your toys and books to other kids. Can you say *why* you did that kind deed? You might be surprised how much your answer matters to God.

Suppose I give everything I have to church or charity, or even half of all I own. You probably would say I was a very good person—a fine Christian. But the apostle Paul said that unless I give because I love, "I am nothing" (1 Corinthians 13:2). Motive matters!

Do you have this kind of love—a love that puts others ahead of yourself? Without Jesus in your heart, you can't have this love. This is the kind of love Jesus had for us when He willingly left the glory of Heaven and went to the cross for our salvation.

Only God can give us a selfless love for others. Will others see the love of Jesus in your life today?

THE SPIRIT OF GOD

"I will ask the Father, and he will give you another Helper.
He will give you this Helper to be with you forever."
JOHN 14:16 ICB

Have you ever wanted to be in two places at the same time? If you're invited to a friend's birthday party on the same day and time as your youth group trip, you can't go to both, no matter how much you want to!

When Jesus went to Heaven, He left us a Helper so that we could have Him with us all the time. Everyone who believes in Jesus can be with Him at every moment. How? Through the Holy Spirit, who lives in the hearts of all who have received Jesus as Savior and Lord. The apostle Paul wrote, "Do you not know . . . that the Spirit of God dwells in you?" (1 Corinthians 3:16).

The Holy Spirit is given to every believer—not for a limited time, but forever! He gives us the gifts and the power we need to live for Jesus. He gives us strength when we are tempted to do wrong. He gives us "love, joy, peace, longsuffering, kindness, goodness, faithfulness, gentleness, self-control" (Galatians 5:22–23).

Wherever you go today, remember that the Holy Spirit, who Jesus called the "Helper," is right there with you!

GETTING OR GIVING?

"Give, and you will receive. You will be given much. . . . The
way you give to others is the way God will give to you."

LUKE 6:38 ICB

Have you ever been invited to give an offering to help children in
need somewhere in the world? Maybe you had been saving your
money to make a special purchase. You had to make a decision to give
to the children in need, or not to give and get the toy you wanted.

Jesus said a lot about giving. Once, He watched people giving their
offerings at the temple. Some rich people gave a lot of money and made
a big show about it. Then a poor woman put in just two tiny coins. Jesus
said that woman gave more than *any* of the rich people, because she
gave all she had to live on (Mark 12:41–44; Luke 21:1–4).

Followers of Jesus should make giving a regular part of their lives.
Jesus said, "Give, and you will receive." If we let go of what we have and
offer it to others, He'll bring us more good in many surprising ways! It's
a promise, and we know Jesus never breaks His promises. Getting . . . or
giving? Which is true of you?

HOW DOES IT WORK?

I know Jesus, the One I have believed in.
2 TIMOTHY 1:12 ICB

Some people ask if Christianity works—does anything really happen when people ask God to forgive their sins and receive Jesus by faith?

I can tell you how it has worked in my own life. I grew up in a Christian home on a farm in North Carolina during a time when a lot of people had no jobs and not much money. My parents weren't able to give me the advantages most young people enjoy today. By the time I was fifteen, I had turned against God, the Bible, and the church.

But one night I committed my life to Jesus, and He gave me a whole new direction. My grades improved. My attitude changed. I began to seek God's will instead of my own way. No, I didn't become perfect, but my life turned around.

I have been all over the world, and I have never met anyone who regretted giving their life to Jesus. And neither will you!

ALWAYS BRIGHT

God is the strength of my heart.
PSALM 73:26

Countries like Finland, Norway, and Sweden have many hours of daylight during the summer—as many as twenty-four hours of sunlight! One visitor in Norway said, "It feels as if you're in paradise, where the lights never go out."

Near the end of the Bible, in the book of Revelation, we find this verse in a description of Heaven: "There shall be no night there: They need no lamp nor light of the sun, for the Lord God gives them light" (22:5). God is love, and He is light.

Any problems we have are opportunities for us to learn more about God's love and His power to help and bless us. When we have confidence in God's promises to always care for us, the brightness of His love will fill our lives.

Don't let problems make you angry or bitter or cause you to lose faith in God. Instead, trust Him as your loving heavenly Father and say, "God is my strength. He is mine forever" (Psalm 73:26 ICB).

NO FEAR

In your lives you must think and act like Christ Jesus.
PHILIPPIANS 2:5 ICB

Some phrases sound alike but have different spellings and different meanings. One example is the saying, "No Christ, Know Fear. Know Christ, No Fear."

We all experience times when we are afraid. Some of us are afraid of the dark or spiders. Some people fear swimming underwater or talking in front of a crowd. If we don't have Jesus in our lives, we're stuck with our fears. But if we know Jesus as our Savior and Friend, we realize that we don't have to be afraid because He is always with us.

Sometimes fear makes us unwilling to talk about our faith. We worry others will laugh at us or reject us. Jesus was never afraid of other people. He knew how and when to speak and when not to. We can learn to follow His example.

Jesus alone is "the way, the truth, and the life" (John 14:6). Never lose your confidence in the truth of the gospel! But—like Jesus—always be "speaking the truth in love" (Ephesians 4:15).

A MIGHTY FORTRESS

He is my refuge and my fortress; my God, in Him I will trust.

PSALM 91:2

Have you ever tried to find the perfect hiding place while playing hide-and-go-seek? Or have you ever put a "Keep Out" sign on the door to your treehouse?

Sometimes in life we look for a safe place too. A *refuge* is a place safely out of harm's way. A *fortress* is a building that can't be broken into by ordinary methods. If friends are pushing us to do something we know is wrong, or if we get a bad illness, we want a refuge or a fortress to keep us safe.

There is a wonderful hymn that says, "A mighty fortress is our God, a bulwark never failing. Our helper He amidst the flood of mortal ills prevailing." This means God is like a shield or a fortress that is stronger than anything we might face. His mighty power can protect us!

Does God care for you and me? Can we turn to Him in trust and faith when troubles and temptations come? Yes—a thousand times yes! He sent His Son, Jesus, to die in our place. What greater proof do we need than that?

COME BOLDLY

"Ask, and it will be given to you; seek, and you will find."
MATTHEW 7:7

Newborn babies can do just one thing for themselves—cry to make their needs known. Whether they are hungry, wet, or cold, babies cry. It's up to the parents to figure out how to take care of them.

As they grow, babies become kids who can talk, and they're not bashful about asking for things. They wouldn't be normal if they didn't boldly make their needs known!

God invites His children to come to Him boldly too. Hebrews 4:16 says, "Let us, then, feel free to come before God's throne. . . . And we can receive mercy and grace to help us" (ICB). Our heavenly Father knows that we depend on Him for our needs. That's why Jesus said, "Ask, and it will be given to you; seek, and you will find; knock, and it will be opened to you" (Matthew 7:7).

Are you facing a problem today? Does your heart feel anxious or worried? Listen: as a child of God, you can turn your worries over to Him, knowing that He loves you and is able to help you. Talk to God about your problems. He wants to hear from you!

GOD'S FOREVER KINGDOM

Your throne, O God, is forever and ever.

PSALM 45:6

Beginning about thirty years before Jesus was born, the Roman Empire ruled for almost five centuries. Leaders of this huge kingdom were called *emperors*. The first was Augustus, and Constantine is one of the most famous. Many other emperors ruled throughout the years, with assistance by kings and governors of smaller territories throughout the empire.

But where is the Roman Empire today? Gone.

Human kingdoms and governments change and disappear, but God's kingdom will last forever. Jesus prayed, "Your kingdom come. Your will be done on earth as it is in heaven" (Matthew 6:10). Wherever God rules in a person's heart, the kingdom of God is there. And someday Jesus will return and set up His kingdom on earth. Finally, He will take us to His kingdom in Heaven.

It may be tomorrow; it may be a thousand years from now. But the outcome is certain—the future belongs to God. And if you belong to the King, you are already royalty in His kingdom that will never end!

MARCH 13

FOR GOD

Stand fast in the Lord.
PHILIPPIANS 4:1

Change is part of everyone's life. We don't always like change. But some changes create new, very valuable results.

A bar of raw steel can be purchased for a few dollars. But when that bar of steel goes into the fire and is formed into tiny springs for expensive watches, it becomes worth thousands of dollars. Fire and the skilled hands of master workers make that steel become much more valuable.

The sun by its heat and light performs a thousand "miracles" a day in the plant kingdom, through the process that God designed. Plants and trees change sunlight into the kinds of energy they need to grow good, healthy food for people all over the world.

People can change for the better too. God through His Spirit changes and refines us. He can take things that seem ordinary to us—our homes, families, talents, education, and even our mistakes and sins—and turn them into something useful, even beautiful, for His purposes. So trust Him, and see what He will do with you!

RESCUING ANGELS

The angel of the LORD encamps all around those
who fear Him, and delivers them.

PSALM 34:7

During World War II, Captain Eddie Rickenbacker and his crew were flying across the Pacific Ocean when they ran out of fuel. Their plane crashed into the water! For three weeks no one heard from them, and across the country thousands of people prayed.

The men had just four oranges with them when the plane went down. After their rescue, Captain Rickenbacker told what they ate next. "A gull came out of nowhere, and lighted on my head——I reached up my hand very gently——I killed him and then we divided him equally among us. We ate every bit. . . . Nothing ever tasted so good." This gull saved them from starvation.

Years later I asked Captain Rickenbacker to tell me the story personally, because it was through this experience that he came to know Jesus. "I have no explanation except that God sent one of His angels to rescue us," he said. He believed wholeheartedly that angels provided the gull!

We may never see them, but God still sends His angels to surround and protect His children——including you and me.

JOYOUS HOPE

My soul shall be joyful in the LORD.
PSALM 35:9

Have you ever experienced a big disappointment? Have you ever lost something that was very important to you? Christians are not promised perfect, trouble-free lives. But Jesus is the answer to our sadness and discouragement, whether our problems are big or small. He can replace them with joy and hope.

Nick Vujicic was born in 1982 without arms or legs. His family loved and cared for him, but as a child and young teen, he struggled with loneliness and fear. Yet God won out! Today Nick fishes, paints, swims, and travels around the world telling others about his faith in Jesus, inviting them to have faith in Him too.

We know God loves us. The Bible says that "nothing can separate us from the love God has for us" (Romans 8:38 ICB). When our confidence is in Him, discouragement gets crowded out. May that be true in your life today!

A SAFE LANDING

"The gate that opens the way to true life is very small. And the
road to true life is very hard. Only a few people find that road."

MATTHEW 7:14 ICB

Once when I was on a flight from Korea to Japan, we ran into a big
snowstorm. When we arrived over the airport in Tokyo, we could
hardly see anything outside the plane windows—just lots of snow—so
the pilot had to land the plane without seeing the runway! I sat up in
the cockpit with him and watched as the controllers in the airport tower
guided him in.

I knew our lives depended on their precise instructions. I did *not*
want them to say to the pilot, "Oh, well, just land any way you want to. We
don't think it'll matter what altitude you keep or how fast you come in."

When we come in for the landing in the great airport of Heaven, we
want to land safely. Sometimes people say that it doesn't really matter
what you believe, that you'll go to Heaven as long as you're sincere.
But Jesus taught that the only way to Heaven is by believing in Him! You
and I can be sure we'll arrive in Heaven safely, because Jesus is our
guide—He has gone before us and made the way.

HAND IT OVER

Give all your worries to him, because he cares for you.
1 PETER 5:7 ICB

Have you ever seen a dump truck get rid of its load? The driver simply pushes a button or pulls on a lever, and the heavy load drops out. A dump truck wasn't made to carry a load forever—it's designed with that giant bucket and special button so it can empty out whatever is inside.

God doesn't want His children to carry around heavy loads of worry or fear. He never wants us to feel crushed under the weight of our concerns! He wants to take on that load for us, because He is strong and because He loves us.

The next time you are anxious or upset, unload your worries on Jesus. You can think of it like pushing the button of faith or pulling the lever of trust and then emptying out your bucket of concerns. Jesus cares about you! He loved you enough to take away the burden of your sins, so you can surely trust Him to handle every other problem as well.

DON'T LOVE MONEY

"What will it profit a man if he gains the whole
world, and loses his own soul?"
MARK 8:36

In the parking lot of a restaurant, eight-year-old Myles Eckert found a twenty-dollar bill lying on the ground. He thought about using it to buy a video game, but then he changed his mind—he saw a soldier in uniform eating lunch with his family. Myles gave the twenty-dollar bill to the soldier with a note, thanking him for his service.

The Bible doesn't say that money or material possessions—games, books, sports equipment, dolls, toys—are bad things. Money and the things we own can do a lot of good when they are used wisely and with the right attitude. The problem, the Bible says, is not with money itself, but with our *love* of money: "The love of money is a root of all kinds of evil" (1 Timothy 6:10).

When we give our money or our favorite things the attention only God deserves, we are growing roots that lead to problems. You might not have much money of your own right now, but you do have possessions. Don't let money, or anything else, take God's rightful place in your life.

MADE NEW

"Unless you are born again, you cannot be in God's kingdom."
JOHN 3:3 ICB

Do you remember the picture book *The Very Hungry Caterpillar*? A tiny caterpillar eats a lot all week until it's time for him to wrap himself up in a cocoon. Two weeks later, the very hungry caterpillar becomes a beautiful butterfly, quite different from who he was before.

Jesus said that if we want to be part of God's kingdom, we must be born again. This new birth is something God does for us when we put our faith and trust in Jesus. So we can come to Jesus with faith and then emerge a new person . . . we can be born again! It sounds incredible, even impossible—and yet it really is what happens. The Bible says, "If anyone belongs to Christ, then he is made new. The old things have gone; everything is made new!" (2 Corinthians 5:17 ICB). We become members of God's family, looking forward to our eternal home in Heaven.

Do you feel like you are in a cocoon, waiting to become a butterfly? Ask Jesus to make you new and grow you into the person He created you to be.

NEW WONDERS EVERY DAY

"The Son gives life to those he wants to."
JOHN 5:21 ICB

As babies grow, they find so much to explore in the world around them. Everything is new—the warmth of the sun, soft green grass, the cheerful chirps of birds. When babies learn to crawl and then walk, they find even more to see and do. Every day is filled with new wonders!

The moment we come to Jesus, we find so much to see and do as well! The Spirit of God brings the life of God into us, and we begin to really live for the first time. There's a bounce in our steps, joy in our souls, and peace in our hearts. There's a whole new direction to our lives, because God is guiding us now. We look forward to discovering what we can do with each new day, week, month, and year of our lives. And we look forward to living forever with God even after we die.

Don't let everyday problems weigh you down. Ask God to help you see His wonders all around you and live each day looking forward to Heaven.

MARCH 21

GOD'S GREAT HEART

"'Love the LORD your God with all your heart' . . .
and 'your neighbor as yourself.'"
LUKE 10:27

Jesus loves me, this I know, for the Bible tells me so." Have you learned this little song? Many of us still love that simple song today, because it reminds us of God's heavenly love for us and for others.

When Jesus lived on earth, He showed love for people in many ways. He cried at the tomb of His friend Lazarus. He mourned over the city of Jerusalem because the people had stopped paying attention to God and His Word. When someone asked Him what the most important commandment was, He replied, "'Love the Lord your God with all your heart.' . . . And the second command is like the first: 'Love your neighbor as you love yourself'" (Matthew 22:37, 39 ICB). His great heart was always sensitive to the needs of others.

Jesus' love was more than human compassion. It was godly love, because Jesus was God. This is the kind of love He calls us to have— and the kind He will give us as we ask Him to help us love others the way He does!

PRAYING FOR GOD TO PROVIDE

Continue praying and keep alert. And when you pray, always thank God.
COLOSSIANS 4:2 ICB

George Müller, born in Germany in the early 1800s, has become well known for how he prayed. Müller became a Christian while he was in college. After he became a pastor and missionary in England, Müller opened an orphanage to take care of the children in need he saw on the streets.

Müller asked God to provide a building, workers, furniture, and money for food and clothing for the children. And God did! Sometimes the answer came at the last minute, but it always came. Müller never asked people for money to run the orphanage. He simply prayed for God to provide whatever was needed that day, and God always prompted people to offer help.

Prayer is a great privilege! Who knows what might happen if millions of believers around the world began to seriously pray for the needs of others? Will you be one of them?

MARCH 23

TURN PROBLEMS TO BLESSINGS

With God's help we will do mighty things.
PSALM 108:13 NLT

Joni Eareckson Tada was just seventeen when she broke her neck on a dive into the Chesapeake Bay. She became paralyzed from the shoulders down. She can't walk or even roll over without help. Since then Joni has used a wheelchair and required much help from others every day. But she has also learned to paint with a brush held in her teeth. She sings and has written books and traveled the world to encourage and help others with disabilities—and to tell people about Jesus.

No one's life is problem-free. Our problems may be big, like Joni's. Or they may be smaller—we are fighting with our siblings or having trouble in school. Sometimes God removes our problems, and it isn't wrong to ask Him to do that. Often He does remove them.

But sometimes the trials remain, and when they do, we should accept them and ask God to teach us from them. We can recognize our troubles as opportunities from God to bless us more than we have ever experienced. How can you use a problem you're having to grow closer to God and help others?

VICTORY BELLS

"I myself am the Lord. I am the only Savior."
ISAIAH 43:11 ICB

A story is told about Easter and the army of French general Napoleon Bonaparte, who conquered much of Europe in the early nineteenth century. The story says that Napoleon's army arrived just outside of an Austrian town called Feldkirch, expecting they'd easily overpower the townspeople the next day. But it was the night before Easter, and the Christians of Feldkirch gathered in their little church to pray.

The next morning at sunrise, the bells of the village rang out across the countryside. Napoleon's army, not realizing it was Easter Sunday, thought that in the night the Austrian army had somehow come into the town, and the bells were ringing for joy. So they decided to leave, and the battle at Feldkirch never took place. The Easter bells caused the enemy to flee, and peace reigned in the Austrian countryside.

As Easter is celebrated each year, church bells all around the world will ring to declare Jesus' victory over death. He is the risen Lord, and because of Him we can live forever in Heaven!

THE ANSWER TO FEAR

"Do not be afraid."
MATTHEW 28:10

O n his TV program *Mister Rogers' Neighborhood*, Fred Rogers often talked with children about fear. Everyone is afraid sometimes, especially when bad things are going on in the world. Mister Rogers suggested that we need to remember the good things that happen, too, and especially the people who try to help.

"When I was a boy," he said, "and I would see scary things in the news, my mother would say to me, 'Look for the helpers. You will always find people who are helping.' To this day, . . . I am always comforted by realizing that there are still so many helpers—so many caring people in this world."

Of course, the most caring Helper we will ever have is Jesus. After Jesus had been put to death, His disciples stayed behind closed doors, filled with fear. But suddenly Jesus was in the room with them! His first words made their fears disappear: "Peace to you" (Luke 24:36). The answer to our fears is found in our faith in the living Lord Jesus.

FEARFUL OR BRAVE?

If God is for us, who can be against us?
ROMANS 8:31

Have you ever had to stand up for what you knew was right? Maybe you chose to be friends with a student other kids made fun of. Maybe you had to walk away from a group that was gossiping or stand up to the class bully.

Or maybe you *wanted* to do the right thing in a situation like these, but you took the easy way out. Even if deep inside we know the right thing to do, sometimes we draw back because we are afraid of the consequences.

How different from the early Christians! From one end of the Roman Empire to the other, they boldly told others about Jesus even when it was dangerous. The apostle Paul said, "God did not give us a spirit that makes us afraid. He gave us a spirit of power and love and self-control" (2 Timothy 1:7 ICB).

We may never face the same dangers those early Christians did. But if we do, let's remember, "If God is for us, who can be against us?"

THE BEST THING ABOUT EASTER

He is not here, but is risen!
LUKE 24:6

What do you like best about Easter? Is it egg hunts, baskets filled with candy, new clothes, sweet baby animals, or beautiful daffodils and lilies?

Easter Sunday is the happiest day on the calendar of the church—and it should be!

For many people, Jesus' resurrection is symbolized by all the traditions of Easter—the signs of spring, new clothes, egg hunts, and Easter baskets. But the best thing about Easter is the news that Jesus is alive! That's the message that makes our faith different from all other religions.

The angel's message is true: "He is not here, but is risen!" And now God's promise is for you: "If you confess with your mouth the Lord Jesus and believe in your heart that God has raised Him from the dead, you will be saved" (Romans 10:9).

PEACE WITH GOD

Let the peace of God rule in your hearts.
COLOSSIANS 3:15

Doctors know that what the Bible taught centuries ago is true—our minds affect the health of our bodies. The book of Proverbs puts it this way: "A cheerful heart is good medicine, but a broken spirit saps a person's strength" (17:22 NLT). Sometimes after a big disappointment, we not only feel sad but also don't have much energy.

Sin affects our minds and our bodies over time, like a poison would. But when Jesus comes into our lives, He removes our guilt. He gives us love for others and a new purpose in life. His joy and peace *neutralize* sin's poison. One dictionary says, "When you neutralize something, you make it harmless or ineffective—usually by applying its opposite force, like pouring water on a fire." That's exactly how Jesus' sacrifice overcomes our sin.

Does that mean all our fears and diseases will vanish? Not necessarily. But God's love will reign in our hearts and give us peace.

CONFIDENCE IN JESUS

Go quickly and tell . . . that He is risen from the dead.
MATTHEW 28:7

The first time you rode your bike without training wheels, the first time you performed in the school play or ran in the track meet, you probably heard someone say, "I have confidence in you! I've seen you practicing. You can do it!" *Confidence* means believing that something can happen because of the evidence you have seen.

We have confidence that we will live forever with Jesus someday because of the evidence that Jesus died on the cross for our sins and rose again on the third day.

On that first resurrection day, the angel at the tomb said, "He is not here; for He is risen" (Matthew 28:6). Sin and death no longer ruled over the human race. Jesus' resurrection changed everything, bringing hope and salvation to all who put their trust in Him.

Listen: If Jesus is your Savior, you can be confident every day that you will live forever with Him in Heaven. That is why the apostle Paul could say, "Thanks be to God, who gives us the victory through our Lord Jesus Christ" (1 Corinthians 15:57).

Is your confidence in Jesus, the risen Lord, today?

JESUS SUFFERED FOR YOU

The punishment, which made us well, was given to him.

ISAIAH 53:5 ICB

Firefighters, police officers, and military men and women all have one thing in common. They are willing to do hard and dangerous things for the benefit of other people.

When Jesus was on the cross, He was in great pain. But Jesus' pain was more than just the physical pain in His body. He also felt the spiritual pain of God's judgment, even though He was the Son of God, perfect and without sin. All our sins were placed on Him, and He suffered and died in our place.

Why did Jesus suffer? Because God loves us. Jesus willingly went to the cross because that was the way He could pay for our sins. The cross is the measure of God's love. How will you respond to His love, poured out on the cross for you?

IT IS FINISHED

He was wounded for the wrong things we did.
ISAIAH 53:5 ICB

On a hill overlooking the harbor of Macao, Portuguese settlers built a massive cathedral. But over time it fell into ruin, except for one wall. On the top of that high, jutting wall, challenging the elements down through the years, was a huge bronze cross.

It is said that a nineteenth-century Englishman saw that cross and was inspired to write these words to a famous hymn: "In the cross of Christ I glory, towering o'er the wrecks of time."

On the cross, just before He died, Jesus lifted up His voice and cried, "It is finished!" (John 19:30). He wasn't referring to His own life, though death was near. Jesus knew that He had successfully completed His mission. His death was paying the penalty for our sins. With the words "It is finished," Jesus announced that Heaven's door was open.

Like the fallen Portuguese cathedral, kingdoms and empires come and go, but the cross and all it stands for will always remain, "towering o'er the wrecks of time."

APRIL

"Let your light so shine before men, that they
may . . . glorify your Father in heaven."
MATTHEW 5:16

JESUS IS ALIVE

It is no longer I who live, but Christ lives in me.
GALATIANS 2:20

At the end of a book or movie, have you ever been surprised by how things turned out? Whatever you thought the ending would be wasn't what happened at all!

Jesus' disciples thought His death was the end of His story—but they were wrong. The very Son of God had come down from Heaven, humbled Himself, and become "obedient to the point of death, even the death of the cross" (Philippians 2:8). As they saw Him die on the cross, the disciples didn't understand that He was dying in the place of sinners. When Jesus had told them that they would see Him again after He died, it didn't make sense to them. They thought everything was over.

But it wasn't! The disciples were so surprised when Jesus rose again, conquering death. If Christ is not alive, there is no hope for any of us. But He is alive! And because He is, "he is able to save completely those who come to God through him, because he always lives to intercede for them" (Hebrews 7:25 NIV). That means that when we ask, Jesus is ready to help you and me. He saves us from our sins, and His power lives within us. That is good news!

YOUR BODY, GOD'S TEMPLE

Do not use your bodies as things to do evil with. . . . Offer the
parts of your body to God to be used for doing good.

ROMANS 6:13 ICB

To have a healthy body, you need to have healthy habits. Eating plenty of vegetables and fruit, *not* eating too much candy and chips, exercising and playing sports, and getting enough sleep help to keep our physical bodies healthy.

The Bible has a lot to say about our bodies. When Jesus is our Savior, He lives within us. Our bodies become dwelling places of the Holy Spirit! The apostle Paul said, "Offer your bodies as living sacrifices, holy and pleasing to God—this is your spiritual act of worship" (Romans 12:1 NIV).

This means that because Jesus sacrificed, or gave, His body for our salvation, the only reasonable thing for us to do is to use our bodies to honor Him. So let me challenge you today to decide to use your body to live for Jesus.

THE RESURRECTION AND THE LIFE

"He who believes in me will live . . . and . . . will never die."
JOHN 11:25–26 NIV

An *enemy* is someone or something that wants to hurt or take away something from another person or country. Sometimes enemies fight battles and wars. And all of us have three great enemies: sin, Satan, and death.

But because Jesus rose from the dead, we know that sin, Satan, and death have been defeated forever. And because Jesus rose from the dead, we know that there is life after death, and that if we belong to Him we don't need to be afraid of death or hell.

Jesus said, "I am the resurrection and the life. He who believes in me will live, even though he dies; and whoever lives and believes in me will never die" (John 11:25–26 NIV). Jesus also promised, "If I go and prepare a place for you, I will come back and take you to be with me that you also may be where I am" (John 14:3 NIV).

These words are true! Jesus rose from the dead, and hundreds of people saw Him alive afterward (1 Corinthians 15:1–8). His resurrection was real. Our great enemies lost and Jesus won! And now we have the wonderful hope of Heaven because of the truth that Jesus is alive!

PURE LIKE GOLD

When He has tested me, I shall come forth as gold.

JOB 23:10

Did you know that gold is found in rocks? It takes a lot of work to get it out—you have to do what's called *refining* work. Chunks of the gold taken out of the rocks are heated until they melt, and when chemicals are added, they cause any other metals mixed in with the gold to separate from it. What's left is pure gold.

Gold becomes more valuable when it is refined and purified. Like gold that must change to become most valuable, our problems can be a way God refines *us* and makes us pure. Our faith in God gets stronger as we see how He takes care of us. Our faith becomes something beautiful and useful to Him, pure like gold.

Our problems can also point us back to the right path. Israel's King David said, "Before I was afflicted I went astray, but now I keep Your word" (Psalm 119:67). Let God use your problems to refine you to be more like Him!

GOD'S UNCHANGING LOVE

O LORD my God, You are very great. . . . You who
laid the foundations of the earth.
PSALM 104:1, 5

Parents love their baby before their baby is even born. They fix up a room, fill a closet and drawers with clothes and blankets, and spend a lot of time just thinking about that special little one they'll meet soon!

God loved us long before today. He loved us before Jesus died on the cross, even before creation began! Before the morning stars sang together, before the first light shone, before the first blades of tender grass peeped out of the earth, God was love. Before God spoke the earth into existence, when it was "without form, and void" (Genesis 1:2), even then God was love.

Before the world was created, God knew all about us. He knew we would need a Savior. So in His love "he chose us in [Jesus] before the creation of the world" (Ephesians 1:4 NIV).

God does not change, and neither does His love. He loved you before you were born, He loves you now, and He will love you forever. Will you love Him in return?

TICKTOCK

As for man, his days are like grass; as a flower
of the field, so he flourishes.
PSALM 103:15

How many clocks does your family have? The first mechanical clocks appeared in Europe in the thirteenth century. Since then, the way clocks are made and the way they work have changed a lot. However we do it, though, people want to keep track of time, and the Bible says that's a good thing to do!

Our lives on earth are actually very short. Instead of wasting time—as we so easily do—God tells us to *redeem* the time. That means to use each day to do good things.

The Bible says God made us in His own image. We each have a soul that will live forever. (Don't let anyone tell you that we are simply a "higher species of animal.") There is a future life with God for those who put their trust in Jesus.

Isn't it wonderful that God wants you to be with Him for all time? Make sure of your relationship to Jesus, and then ask God to help you live each day for Him.

BE GENEROUS

The generous soul will be made rich.
PROVERBS 11:25

What is the best present you've ever received? Was it a special birthday or Christmas present you had asked for? Or was it a complete surprise—a gift you weren't expecting at all?

What is the best gift you have ever *given* to someone else?

Jesus taught that "it is more blessed to give than to receive" (Acts 20:35). The Bible teaches that blessings follow those who give liberally. Proverbs 11:25 says, "The generous soul will be made rich, and he who waters will also be watered himself." But sometimes we are afraid to be generous. We are afraid we won't have enough left over.

When people decide to tithe (to give a tenth of their income), however, they discover what so many others have learned too: you can't outgive God. He will always provide for you.

What keeps you from being more generous in supporting God's work? Why not discover the blessing of giving generously? You could give some money to your church, some clothes to a donation center, or some of your time to help a neighbor with yardwork. Remember, "God loves a cheerful giver" (2 Corinthians 9:7).

GOD CARES FOR YOU

God is not the author of confusion but of peace.
1 CORINTHIANS 14:33

Have you ever been punished by your mom or dad for something you did wrong and thought, *It's not fair!* Maybe you even wondered if your parents really love you. How could they take your video games or something else you enjoy if they love you? How could they make you miss playing with your friends if they love you?

Well, it's actually not too hard to answer to those questions. Your parents discipline you to teach you—*because* they love you.

Sometimes people ask, "Does God really love me?" In the Bible, Martha said to Jesus, "Lord, do You not care?" (Luke 10:40).

That question is forever answered in these reassuring words from the apostle Peter: "He cares for you" (1 Peter 5:7). You can be sure that God cares for you. If He didn't, would He have sent Jesus to die for you? Of course not! That is why you can always turn to Him for the strength and encouragement you need in any situation. God knows what you are facing, and "He cares for you."

THE GOOD SHEPHERD

"The good shepherd lays down his life for the sheep."
JOHN 10:11 NIV

Sheep can't take care of themselves. Without someone looking after them, they'll eat pasture grasses down to the bare ground, drink dirty water, and become prey for wild animals. Sheep are easily upset, frightened, and distracted. They don't know how to find their way back to the flock if they wander off.

Jesus is our Good Shepherd. The Bible says, "We are His people and the sheep of His pasture" (Psalm 100:3). He takes care of us like a shepherd cares for his sheep. Jesus said, "I am the good shepherd. The good shepherd lays down his life for the sheep. . . . I know my sheep and my sheep know me" (John 10:11, 14 NIV).

Like a shepherd guards sheep, Jesus guards us. He never runs away when we have a problem. He knows each of us by name and calls us so we can follow Him. And Jesus gave His life to save us. Because we belong to Jesus, the Good Shepherd, we can be secure and at rest.

THE MESSAGE OF EASTER

He has risen! He is not here.

MARK 16:6 NIV

Have you ever looked carefully at the wheels on a bike or a car? If you do, you'll see that they work by moving around a piece in their center called an *axle*. Whenever you're pedaling your bike or riding in the car, those axles make all the difference in helping you travel safely.

Like that important axle at the center of the wheel, the important message of Easter is at the center of Christianity. And the message of Easter is that Jesus is alive!

The apostle Paul said, "If Christ has not been raised, then your faith is for nothing; you are still guilty of your sins" (1 Corinthians 15:17 ICB). It is that simple. If Jesus is still dead, then He cannot be our Savior. But Jesus *is* risen! That's what the Bible teaches and what hundreds of witnesses reported that they saw.

What does Easter mean to you? It should mean everything, because Jesus conquered death! And that makes all the difference—now and forever!

JESUS IS COMING BACK

This same Jesus, who has been taken from you into heaven, will come back in the same way you have seen him go into heaven.
ACTS 1:11 NIV

When someone we love has been away and comes back, what do we do? We celebrate! It might be a mom or dad in the military who comes home after a long overseas service, or a big sister who comes home from college for the summer, or a grandparent who moved far away but comes back for a visit. When people we love come back to us, we're joyful!

Jesus told His disciples that He will come back. Forty days after the resurrection, the disciples watched Jesus go up into Heaven on a cloud. Then two angels reminded them that Jesus will return: "Men of Galilee, . . . why do you stand here looking into the sky? This same Jesus, who has been taken from you into heaven, will come back in the same way you have seen him go into heaven" (Acts 1:11 NIV).

Yes, Jesus will come back! He made that promise. Just as He rose from the dead, He will return and take us to Heaven with Him. Every promise He made—no exceptions!—will come true.

YOU CAN COUNT ON IT

"Blessed is the man who trusts in the LORD, and whose hope is the LORD."

JEREMIAH 17:7

B elieving and obeying Jesus is like building a house on a strong, solid foundation. Maybe you have sung the song about the wise man who built his house upon the rock and the foolish man who built his house upon the sand. Or maybe you've heard the old hymn that begins, "My hope is built on nothing less, than Jesus' blood and righteousness; I dare not trust the sweetest frame, but wholly lean on Jesus' name. On Christ, the solid Rock, I stand; all other ground is sinking sand."

Even the things we count on every day——like lights that go on when we flip the switch and water to drink when we turn on the faucet——even these usually reliable things can let us down. And the things we hope for sometimes——like a special birthday gift or an award in a contest—— these hopes might not come true. But the greatest hope of all is our hope of salvation in Jesus——and *that* hope is an absolute certainty, because it is based completely on "Jesus' blood and righteousness"—— His sacrifice for us.

The greatest hope of all is one we can count on!

WHY DID JESUS DIE?

The message of the cross . . . is the power of God.
1 CORINTHIANS 1:18

God created a perfect world of amazing beauty. He walked in the garden with Adam and Eve, the first man and woman. He talked with them. Everything should've been wonderful—and it was until sin came into the world. When Adam and Eve disobeyed God and ate from the Tree of Knowledge of Good and Evil, everything changed. From then on, all people—except Jesus—have sinned.

Sin is the reason that Jesus, the Son of God, was crucified. Not Pilate, not Judas, not the angry mob—but sin. All the bad and sad things that happen in the world are the results of a world poisoned by sin.

And that is why Jesus died. All our sins sent Him to the cross. Jesus prayed in His last hours, "My Father, if it is possible, do not give me this cup of suffering. But do what you want, not what I want" (Matthew 26:39 ICB). There was no way other than the cross. Why did He take on that awful punishment? So you and I would not have to. Only one power in the world is greater than sin—the power of God's love.

FORGIVING AND FORGETTING

"I will forgive their iniquity, and their sin I will remember no more."

JEREMIAH 31:34

Have you ever forgotten to take your lunch or your homework to school? Or forgotten to clean your room or walk the dog? We all forget important things sometimes.

Even God forgets—but His forgetting is different from ours. While we don't mean to forget things, God *chooses* not to remember our sins after He has forgiven us.

This is why we must come to the cross, asking God to forgive our sins and trusting Jesus alone to save us. We have to admit that we are sinners and that we can't save ourselves. Then God gives Jesus' righteousness—His perfect life—to us. He forgives us because of Jesus, and "those who are in Christ Jesus are not judged guilty" (Romans 8:1 ICB). Because of Jesus, God chooses to forget our sin, and we can spend eternity with Him in Heaven.

APRIL 15

HEAVENLY NEWS

God both raised up the Lord and will also raise us up by His power.
1 CORINTHIANS 6:14

Before there were TVs, the Internet, or cell phones, people depended on newspapers to give them the news of the day. In big cities newsboys stood on street corners to sell the daily paper to people walking by. If something especially important happened, the newspaper put out an extra edition with the story, and the newsboys shouted, "Extra! Extra! Read all about it!"

The angel who came to the garden, where Jesus' body lay, rolled away the stone from the empty tomb. When a group of women arrived at the tomb, they heard the amazing news: "He is not here, but is risen!" (Luke 24:6). Talk about news worth shouting about!

Jesus' resurrection took away our fears of death. The angel's words and the empty tomb tell us about the wonderful power of the living God. What wonderful, heavenly news!

Jesus' promise has been fulfilled: "Because I live, you will live also" (John 14:19).

THE GREATEST MESSAGE

I know that you seek Jesus who was crucified.
He is not here; for He is risen.
MATTHEW 28:5–6

The greatest message the world has ever heard are the words spoken by an angel sitting outside Jesus' empty tomb: "He is not here; for He is risen." These few words changed the history of the universe.

The Bible says that on the third day after Christ's death, "there was a great earthquake; for an angel of the Lord descended from heaven, and came and rolled back the stone from the door, and sat on it. His countenance was like lightning, and his clothing as white as snow. And the guards shook for fear of him, and became like dead men" (Matthew 28:2–4).

A woman named Mary looked into the tomb and saw "two angels in white sitting, one at the head and the other at the feet, where the body of Jesus had lain" (John 20:12). Then one of the angels who was sitting outside the tomb proclaimed the greatest message the world has ever heard! Darkness and despair died; hope and anticipation were born in the hearts of men!

Jesus didn't stay in the manger . . . or on the cross . . . or in the tomb. He is alive, and even now He wants to walk beside you every day!

NEVER STOP PRAYING

We have not stopped praying for you.
COLOSSIANS 1:9 NLT

For twenty years, Harriet prayed for three boys who lived on her street. She wanted them to know Jesus. Even though she didn't see any results from her prayers, she kept on praying, year after year.

When one of the boys grew up and went to college, there was a day when he felt drawn into a Christian bookstore. He bought a Bible and began to read it. Soon he started attending a church near his home and gave his life to Jesus. It was the same church that Harriet attended! How thankful she was that she had kept on praying! And today that young man is a pastor, author, and speaker for God and for the gospel.

The Bible says, "Never stop praying" (1 Thessalonians 5:17 ICB). As a follower of Jesus, make this your motto. Never stop praying, no matter how impossible a situation may seem. Our responsibility isn't to tell God when He must act or even how He must act. Our responsibility is simply to keep on praying and trusting Him to act according to His perfect will.

ASKING AND ANSWERING

My God shall supply all your need.
PHILIPPIANS 4:19

What is the biggest thing you have ever asked for? A bike? For someone to forgive you? Did you know Jesus told His followers that they could ask for anything and receive it? Here is His promise: "If you remain in me and my words remain in you, you may ask for anything you want, and it will be granted!" (John 15:7 NLT).

Wait a minute. Doesn't God sometimes answer prayers with "no" or "not now"? Does this verse mean God promises to give us *anything* we want, anytime? No. God loves us too much to answer prayers that are foolish or might harm us. Sometimes He answers "no" or "not now" because He has something better to give you. But the more we stay close to Him and let His Word into our hearts, the more we want what *He* wants. Our prayers become more and more about what is important to Him.

The Bible says, "The Lord will withhold no good thing from those who do what is right" (Psalm 84:11 NLT). You can trust that promise!

SHINING LIGHTS

"Let your light so shine before men, that they
may . . . glorify your Father in heaven."
MATTHEW 5:16

Jesus told His disciples to let their light shine so that more and more people could know and praise God. What did He mean?

Light lets us see in the dark. When a storm brings down electric wires and the power goes out in our homes, we light candles so we can see as we walk from room to room. When a ship needs help to navigate at night, the strong light from a lighthouse guides the way. And the good lives of Christians are like light to other people who need to find their way to God.

The first-century Christians became known for their good lives and how they loved their neighbors. Their example of compassion and good deeds attracted others to believe in Jesus too.

If we try to hide our light, that's like putting a lamp under a barrel . . . it doesn't help anyone.

But we'll influence the world around us in wonderful ways when we let Jesus' light shine in our lives. What do others see in your life that draws them to Jesus?

YOKED

"Take My yoke upon you and learn from Me."

MATTHEW 11:29

Jesus calls us to follow Him and obey Him. Does this sound too hard to do? Actually, it would be *impossible* to do if we didn't have His help.

That's why Jesus said, "Take My yoke upon you and learn from Me, for I am gentle and lowly in heart, and you will find rest for your souls. For My yoke is easy and My burden is light" (Matthew 11:29–30). What does it mean to be "yoked with Jesus"?

In Bible times farmers plowed their lands with a pair of oxen, joined together with a wooden collar, or *yoke*, that fit around their necks. To be yoked is to be connected, side by side. To be "yoked with Jesus" means to learn to walk with Him, learning His ways and letting Him lead. It's *His* yoke, remember?

Following and obeying Jesus isn't always easy, but it can always be a joy—because now we are yoked to God's own Son, and He makes heavy burdens light.

Today are you yoked with the world or with Jesus?

APRIL 21

GOD NEVER CHANGES

"I am the LORD, I do not change."
MALACHI 3:6

Have you ever seen a photo of your parents or grandparents taken when they were in high school or college? Did you have trouble recognizing them? Not only were they younger than they are now, but they probably had very different hair and clothing styles too! You might have had a good laugh about how everyone was dressed.

People change and fashions change. Conditions and circumstances change, but God never changes. God has no beginning and no ending, and He is unchangeable—He is always the same. The Bible says, "Every good action and every perfect gift is from God. These good gifts come down from the Creator of the sun, moon, and stars. God does not change like their shifting shadows" (James 1:17 ICB).

God's love never changes. His holiness never changes. His purpose never changes. His glory never changes. He is the same yesterday, today, and forever.

Can you think of any reason not to trust Him? Neither can I!

THE HOPE OF THE CENTURIES

It is good that one should hope and wait
quietly for the salvation of the LORD.
LAMENTATIONS 3:26

What is the most spectacular event you've ever seen in the sky? Was it a brilliant sunset or a double rainbow? Maybe it was a gleaming jet zooming overhead or an eagle with its wings spread wide, soaring high above the trees.

Someday the world will look up and see the most glorious sight that ever will be seen—the promised second coming of Jesus. The Bible says, "The Lord Himself will descend from heaven with a shout, with the voice of an archangel, and with the trumpet of God" (1 Thessalonians 4:16). It also tells us that He'll be "coming with clouds" and that "every eye will see Him" (Revelation 1:7). The second coming of Jesus has been the great hope of believers in every century.

Someday the King will return. Someday the heavens will shout, "The kingdoms of this world have become the kingdoms of our Lord and of His Christ, and He shall reign forever and ever!" (Revelation 11:15). Jesus alone is the answer of hope for the world!

APRIL 23

COMFORTING OTHERS

Comfort each other and give each other strength.
1 THESSALONIANS 5:11 ICB

Little children like to have a favorite stuffed animal or blanket with them as they go to sleep—or sometimes take with them wherever they go! Everyone needs comforting sometimes.

When you are disappointed or sad, what comforts you? Has anyone ever said or done something for you that really helped you feel better? Usually it is people who have had the same kind of problems or disappointments we are having who can comfort us the most. This also means that we can learn from our troubles and use what we learn to comfort someone else who is going through the same thing!

If we learn from our problems, then we can understand the troubles of others because of what we've experienced in our own lives.

So when disappointments and problems come, don't just hope they will pass as quickly as possible. Instead, trust God and try to learn all you can from the experience so that someday you can comfort and encourage someone else!

WALK WITH GOD DAILY

My eyes shall be on the faithful of the land, that they may dwell with me.

PSALM 101:6

Football practice. Art lessons. Piano practice. Rehearsal for the school play. Whatever you want to be good at, you have to practice doing it. It's the same with your Christian faith. How you live your daily life *now* prepares you for how you will serve God in the future.

Noah had a close relationship with God, and when the flood came, God chose Noah to build the ark and saved him. Moses lived many years in the solitude of the desert, which helped prepare him to lead the Israelites out of Egypt to the promised land. As a shepherd boy, David loved and followed God; when he was called to rule his people, he was prepared to be king. Daniel stayed faithful to God during the years he was forced to serve a foreign king; when the lions' den came, he was ready.

God has not promised to deliver us from trouble, but He has promised to go through it with us and help us use it as practice for the future. So we can say, "Even if I walk through a very dark valley, I will not be afraid because you are with me" (Psalm 23:4 ICB).

THE CROWN OF LIFE

Blessed is the man who endures trial, for . . .
he will receive the crown of life.
JAMES 1:12 RSV

In most contests there's just one winner. Only one person gets the first place trophy or the crown.

But every faithful Christian will someday receive the crown of life. The apostle Paul said, "There is laid up for me the crown of righteousness, which the Lord, the righteous Judge, will give to me on that Day, and not to me only but also to all who have loved His appearing" (2 Timothy 4:8).

To the Christian, death is said in the Bible to be a coronation. The picture here is that of a regal prince who, after his struggles and conquests in an alien land, returns to his native country and court to be crowned and honored for his deeds.

The day Paul is talking about in that verse is the day we enter Heaven. The Bible says we are pilgrims and strangers in a foreign land. This world is not our home; our citizenship is in Heaven. And someday all our battles on this earth will be over, and we will enter that heavenly home.

Never forget: if you are a Christian, you are a child of the King, and there is a crown waiting for you!

NOW IS THE TIME

You do not know what will happen tomorrow.

JAMES 4:14

H as anyone ever asked you, "What do you want to be when you grow up?" What was your answer? Maybe you said a firefighter, preacher, teacher, or musician. The important thing is to have ideas and try some things out. We have to start training and practicing to become what we want to be when we grow up.

It's the same with living for Jesus. There's no reason to say that we will serve Jesus *someday*, when we're older. Even children can serve Jesus! And you can start today. Then you will never need to look back on a lifetime—or even a day—of wasted opportunities.

Do you want to know God's Word better, talk to Him more, or tell others about Jesus' love? Do you want to help others in need? There's no better time to begin than right now!

CHRIST IS KING

Your kingdom is an everlasting kingdom.
PSALM 145:13

The United States began as colonies ruled by England. Eventually the colonists rebelled—they wanted to be able to govern, or rule, themselves as a nation of independent states. The Declaration of Independence was signed in 1776, and a new democracy began.

The word *democracy* means "rule by the people." But no democracy can ever be better than the people who make it up. When the people are wise and participate in government, democracy works well. When citizens are selfish, lazy, or dishonest, the government will be the same. When everyone wants his own way, someone is going to get hurt.

The government in God's kingdom is not a democracy where the people govern, but a *Christocracy*—where Jesus is the supreme authority. In God's kingdom, Jesus is King. He is compassionate, fair, merciful, and just, and because of His death and resurrection, He is worthy to direct the kingdom and all His followers.

Is Jesus the King of your life today?

GOD'S DOWN PAYMENT

He . . . put his Spirit in our hearts as a deposit,
guaranteeing what is to come.

2 CORINTHIANS 1:21—22 NIV

When a family wants to buy a house, they usually must make a *down payment*, which is a portion of the total price of the house. Making a down payment means the family is serious about buying the house. They are making a promise to pay the rest of the price over time. The down payment allows them to move into the house and live there—even though it still belongs to the bank until the full price is paid.

In New Testament times, a down payment was known as a *deposit* or *pledge*. And the Bible says that as we trust in Jesus, God gives us the Spirit "in our hearts as a deposit, guaranteeing what is to come." Putting the Holy Spirit in our hearts is God's down payment to us. It is a *seal*, or sign, that He is serious about saving us. It is a promise that someday our salvation will be complete. And it gives us the right to enjoy being God's child today and every day from now on!

APRIL 29

LIVE FOR THE LORD

My days are swifter than a weaver's shuttle.
JOB 7:6

My home state of North Carolina is known for making fabrics. I have visited the textile mills and watched the giant looms weaving cloth from colorful thread. The shuttles that weave the thread on the looms move like lightning—they're so fast they're almost impossible to see.

In the Old Testament, Job said that his days were "swifter than a weaver's shuttle." When we are young, the years seem to move slowly, but older people realize that life passes quickly. It's almost over before we realize it. The reason, according to the Bible, is eternity. Though we live to be seventy, eighty, or ninety years old, that is but a snap of the finger compared to eternity.

Our world seems to like things that go fast. Race cars. Baseball pitches. Olympic track stars. Rocket ships. Let's remember that our lives go fast, too, and live them for the Lord.

THE SECRET OF PURITY

Who may go up on the mountain of the Lord? . . .
Only those with clean hands and pure hearts.

PSALM 24:3—4 ICB

D o you have friends who are allowed to do things you're not allowed to do? Maybe some of your friends watch movies and listen to music your family doesn't. Perhaps your parents have explained that your family's rules are for your protection.

We live in a society that seems to allow impure and bad behavior more and more all the time. "If it feels good, do it" has become the motto. But that is not God's way.

Many Christian men and women have done things they're not proud of—they committed crimes or did things they knew were wrong. We rejoice with them that Jesus has redeemed and forgiven them. Yet they will tell you that they wish they'd never fallen into such sin. How much better to have avoided sin in the first place! God's standard has not changed: "You shall be holy, for I the Lord your God am holy" (Leviticus 19:2).

The secret of purity is God. When we are committed to Jesus, we will seek a pure heart—a heart cleansed by the Holy Spirit and the Word of God.

MAY

If we confess our sins, He is faithful and
just to forgive us our sins.
1 JOHN 1:9

GOD'S KIND OF STRENGTH

They shall walk and not faint.
ISAIAH 40:31

People and nations put their security in weapons, expecting their guns and tanks and missiles to keep them safe. But have the world's weapons brought us lasting security? No. I am reminded of the false prophets of Jeremiah's day: "They give assurances of peace when there is no peace" (Jeremiah 8:11 NLT).

Christians, however, can always have peace. Whether you are up against an unkind student at your school, the opposing soccer team, or the struggles of poverty or war, peace comes from putting our trust in the living God. These words of the prophet Isaiah still speak to us today: "Those who wait on the Lord shall renew their strength; . . . they shall walk and not faint" (Isaiah 40:31). The strength and presence of God with us gives us peace no matter what the circumstances.

GOD'S LOVE

Great is the LORD, and greatly to be praised.

PSALM 48:1

When I was growing up in the rural South, my idea of the ocean was so small. The first time I saw the Atlantic Ocean, I couldn't imagine how any body of water could be so big! The size of the ocean can't be understood until you've seen it.

The same is true about God's love. Until you actually experience it, no one can fully describe its wonders to you. You may recall a song you learned called "Deep and Wide." God's love is deep and wide—deeper than you can see and wider than you can reach.

God's love is shown in everything He does and in everything about Him. One quality of God is called His *omniscience*—His ability to know and understand all things. Only God knows everything all at the same time. At all times, we can realize that God knows, loves, watches, understands, and, more than that, has a purpose. Never forget: God's love for you is deep and wide and can never run out!

MAY 3

WALK WITH GOD

Walk in the Spirit, and you shall not fulfill the lust of the flesh.
GALATIANS 5:16

To walk means to place one foot in front of the other and to go forward one step at a time. If you stop doing this, you are no longer walking. You are standing still—or worse, going backward. *Walking* always implies movement, progress, and direction. Walking with God is a little like following the directions of a GPS in a car. It means moving forward according to His directions, knowing that where He's leading is where you want to go.

The problem is that we are weak. We stop moving in God's direction and start going other directions, away from Him, instead. This happens when we do something unkind, for example, or if we tell a lie or take something from a store without paying for it.

But that is one reason why the Holy Spirit has been given to us. The Spirit guides us *and* gives us strength to follow God's directions!

One of the highest compliments in the Bible is found in these words about Noah: "Noah was a just man, perfect in his generations. Noah walked with God" (Genesis 6:9). Could this be said of us?

FOLLOW GOD'S PLAN

Be transformed . . . that you may prove what
is that . . . perfect will of God.
ROMANS 12:2

D o you like to bake or cook? What's your favorite thing to make? It's important to follow the recipe carefully if you want the food to turn out well. Have you ever had food where the cook put in too much salt or too little sugar, or forgot to put in one ingredient? How did the food taste?

The Bible shows us that God has a recipe—a plan—for everyone, and that if we are following Him day by day, that "recipe" will turn out just right.

God does not reveal His plan through fortune-telling or any kind of hocus-pocus. His perfect will is reserved for those who have trusted Jesus for salvation and who humbly seek His will for their lives.

We cannot know the will of God for our lives unless we first come to the cross and confess that we are sinners and receive Jesus as Lord and Savior. Once you do come to Him, you begin a whole new life—a life lived not for yourself, but for Christ. From that moment on, God wants to show you His will. Whatever decisions you face today, ask God to guide you and follow as He leads.

MAY 5

GONE FOR GOOD

If we confess our sins, He is faithful and just to forgive us our sins.
1 JOHN 1:9

Corrie ten Boom told a story about a little girl who broke one of her mother's china cups. The little girl came crying to her mother and said, "Oh, Mama, I'm so sorry I broke your beautiful cup!"

"I know you're sorry, and I forgive you," the mother said kindly. "There's no need to cry anymore." Then she swept up the pieces of the broken cup and put them in the trash.

But the little girl still felt bad. She went to the trash can, picked out pieces of the broken cup, and brought them to her mother again. "Oh, Mama," she said again, "I'm so sorry that I broke your pretty cup!"

This time her mother spoke firmly to her. "Put those pieces back in the trash, and don't take them out again. I told you I forgave you!"

If we have confessed our sins to Jesus, we don't need to keep holding on to our guilt. God has forgiven us and taken our sins away—forever!

SMALL BUT MIGHTY

When I am weak, then I am strong.
2 CORINTHIANS 12:10

You might be surprised to learn about the strength of a tiny, ordinary ant. Ants have been seen hauling bits of food and even small pebbles back to their colonies. In fact, ants can lift and carry up to fifty times their own body weight! Their small size doesn't mean they are weak.

The apostle Paul could say, "When I am weak, then I am strong," because the Lord had told him, "My strength is made perfect in weakness" (2 Corinthians 12:9). Only when Paul admitted his own weakness and was willing to get out of the way could God take over and work.

If we try to do God's will in our own strength, then we can take the credit for whatever gets done. But when we let God's strength work through our weakness, then He will get the glory—and that is as it should be.

So the next time you have to do something that is hard for you, admit your weakness. Maybe it's hard to obey your parents, or do your homework, or be kind to the new kid at school. Tell God your weakness, and ask Him to make you strong with His strength.

THIRSTY

My soul thirsts for God, for the living God.
PSALM 42:2

Think of a time when you were really, really thirsty. What drink did you want most? Most people in that situation would answer, "Water." Our bodies are made up largely of water, and if we don't have enough water to drink, the cells and organs of our bodies can't do their jobs.

The first verse of Psalm 42 says, "As the deer longs for streams of water, so I long for you, O God" (NLT). When deer are thirsty, they want water. Water is the only thing that will quench their thirst.

Just like our bodies need water, our souls need God. Even the best things in life, whatever makes us happiest, can't be enough for us for very long. Only God can meet our deepest desires.

Don't let anything—or anyone—come between you and God. The prophet Isaiah wrote, "Why spend your money on something that is not real food? Why work for something that doesn't really satisfy you?" (Isaiah 55:2 ICB). What in your life might be crowding out a desire to be close with God?

God wants you to know Him in a personal way, and He has made this possible through Jesus Christ. He loves you!

TUNING IN

God . . . has in these last days spoken to us by His Son.
HEBREWS 1:1—2

When I was a boy, there was no TV or Internet. In fact, radio was a new development and just becoming popular! My family would gather around our simple radio and turn the dials. Often the only sound we heard was the squeak and squawk of static. But we knew that somewhere out there a transmitter was sending sound over the airwaves, and if we could tune in to the right radio station, we could hear a voice loud and clear.

Does God speak to us? Is He trying to reach us? Yes! If we're not hearing Him, it's because we're not tuned in.

There is only one way we could have ever known God: if He revealed Himself to us. And He has—in the wonderful world He created and in His written Word, the Bible. Centuries ago He spoke to the prophets and the apostles, and guided by the Holy Spirit, they wrote down His Word for us.

God wants to speak to us—we just need to tune in to His Word. Are you listening?

MAY 9

GOD'S SECRET SERVANTS

He will give his angels charge of you to guard you in all your ways.
PSALM 91:11 RSV

In the late 1800s, German composer Engelbert Humperdinck and his sister wrote a musical version of the fairy tale "Hansel and Gretel" that is still performed today. Early in the opera, Hansel and Gretel become lost at night in a dangerous forest. Before they finally fall asleep, they sing their evening prayers, and fourteen angels come to surround them and keep them safe throughout the night.

Angels are God's secret servants. They never fail at the tasks God gives them. Often when people talk or write about angels, they don't base their beliefs on what the Bible says about angels. But angels *are* real, and God has commanded them to watch over us. They are usually unseen and unrecognized, and only in Heaven will you know everything they did to keep you safe. In the meantime, you can be glad about their presence, and thank God for the ways He loves and protects through His secret servants, the angels.

IN JESUS' PRESENCE

The upright shall dwell in Your presence.

PSALM 140:13

I f you could meet any important person living in the world today, who would it be? A singer or musician? A sports star? The president? What would you do if you were about to meet this person? I'm sure you would want to dress well and know ahead of time what you might say or do.

Someday you and I will meet the most important person ever: Jesus, the King of kings. The Bible says we'll be dressed in white robes (Revelation 7:9). In His presence we will bow in humble worship and praise. And like those who are at His throne now, we will say, "You are worthy, O Lord, to receive glory and honor and power" (Revelation 4:11).

Are you prepared for that day when you will meet the King of kings face-to-face? No one knows the day or the hour when life will end. The time for you to prepare is now, by committing your life to Jesus and beginning to live as a child of the King.

MAY 11

HOW TO GET STRONGER

Blessed is the man whom You instruct, O Lord.
PSALM 94:12

You probably know that we develop muscles as we exercise. Sitting on the couch watching TV or playing video games won't develop muscles! Did you know that the heart is a muscle too? To have a strong heart, the American Heart Association recommends sixty minutes of exercise every day.

The Bible tells us that we become stronger *spiritually* only through exercise too—through using our spiritual "muscles" to meet our challenges and problems. One reason God allows suffering to come to His people, the Bible says, is to teach us and mold us.

C. S. Lewis, the author of The Chronicles of Narnia, said, "We have no right to happiness; only an obligation to do our duty." Sometimes our spiritual exercise will include hard things. When it does, ask God to teach you and make you strong as you go through it with Him. Remember, "Blessed is the man whom You instruct, O Lord."

A NEW CREATION

If anyone is in Christ, he is a new creation; old things have passed away.

2 CORINTHIANS 5:17

In the movie *The Wizard of Oz,* Dorothy meets a scarecrow looking for a brain, a lion looking for courage, and a tin man looking for a heart. The Wizard of Oz promises he can provide what they're looking for—but in the end, he disappoints them. He gives gifts to Dorothy's friends that stand for the brains, courage, and heart they want, but that's all he can do. He can't make them completely new.

The Bible says our old sinful nature must be changed to a new nature, and that is exactly what God is ready and able to do. He says, "I will give you a new heart and put a new spirit within you" (Ezekiel 36:26).

What a challenge! We can't change ourselves in our own strength. And no other human can do it for us either.

But God can! "If anyone is in Christ, he is a new creation." God can make us completely new people who are like Jesus! He wants to come into our lives and begin to change us from within. Have you asked Him to do that? He will!

KINGDOM AMBASSADORS

We are ambassadors for Christ, as though God were pleading through us.
2 CORINTHIANS 5:20

What do Benjamin Franklin and former president George H. W. Bush have in common? They both served as ambassadors from the United States to other countries. What are *ambassadors*? They are representatives and servants of their government in a foreign land. Ambassadors aren't free to set their own policies or develop their own messages. Instead, they are sent to communicate and carry out the will of the governments they represent. In other words, an ambassador is a person under authority.

In the Bible, the apostle Paul called Christians ambassadors for Christ. We live under the authority of Jesus and the authority of the Bible, the Word of God. We are servants, and our job is to tell others about Jesus. We must do the will of God, not whatever we want.

The world today is looking for holy men and women who live under the authority of the Word of God. People will not listen to what we say unless we back it up with the way we live. Are you a faithful ambassador for Christ to those around you?

A BETTER LIFE

Have quiet and peaceful lives—lives full of worship and respect for God.

1 TIMOTHY 2:2 ICB

Have you ever had a perfect day? What made that day perfect? Most of us would say that a perfect day is filled with lots of good things and nothing bad.

The world we live in isn't perfect. Christians are part of society, and we have problems and difficulties just like everyone else.

The Bible says a lot about our responsibility to help others. Jesus said, "Do for other people the same things you want them to do for you" (Matthew 7:12 ICB). You can speak up for someone who is being teased or bullied. You can donate some of your own money or clothes to help others after a flood or tornado. You can raise money or supplies for medical mission trips. There's so much that any of us can do!

God loves our hurting world. Jesus saw the crowds and "was moved with compassion for them, because they were weary" (Matthew 9:36). We want to do all we can to help others enjoy peace and dignity.

Jesus is concerned about meeting all the needs of each person in each community. Do we share His concern? How can you help?

TWO GIFTS IN ONE

The kingdom of God is . . . righteousness and
peace and joy in the Holy Spirit.
ROMANS 14:17

You can't make toast for breakfast if the toaster's not plugged in. The toaster was designed and built to run on electricity. If it's not plugged into an electric outlet, it is still a toaster, but it has no power to turn bread into toast.

God made us, and He makes us His children when we accept His great gift of forgiveness. But just like the toaster needs electricity to be able to toast bread, we need power to be able to live the way God says we should. So God offers us the great gift of the Holy Spirit—He is our power source! He gives us the power to be truly good as we yield ourselves to Him.

Everyone who wants to follow Jesus and live for Him needs this two-sided gift God offers: First, we need Jesus' work *for* us by dying on the cross for our sins. Second, we need the Holy Spirit's work *in* us. This is how God answers our desire for forgiveness *and* for goodness. As a friend of mine has said, "I need Jesus Christ for my eternal life, and the Holy Spirit of God for my internal life." He might have added, ". . . so I can live my external life to the fullest."

GOD AT WORK

"Blessed are those who have not seen and yet have believed."
JOHN 20:29

Early in the twentieth century, Robert Ripley began creating a daily cartoon feature called *Ripley's Believe It or Not.* The feature continues today, filled with unbelievable-but-true facts about people, animals, and events—like Nora, a cat in New Jersey who taught herself to play the piano!

Sometimes it's hard to see that God is at work in our lives. In the Old Testament, the prophet Habakkuk complained to God that evil people were getting away with doing bad things. But God answered, "I will work a work in your days which you would not believe, though it were told you" (Habakkuk 1:5).

Robert Ripley reported strange stories that people could choose to believe—or not. Today people can choose to believe God's Word or not. For thousands of years, people of faith have believed God and discovered that His Word *is* true. We can believe that God really is the Ruler over everything and that He is at work, even if we can't see it.

God is at work, even in the midst of the problems and frustrations of our day. He alone is God—and that's why we can trust Him.

CONFIDENCE AND PEACE

You will keep him in perfect peace, whose mind is stayed on You.
ISAIAH 26:3

M any times when I meet Jewish friends, I greet them by saying *Shalom*, the Hebrew word for "peace." And often when I greet my Arab friends, I use their word for "peace," *Salam*. It shows them that I want to be their friend and that I wish them good things like peace.

When we are peaceful, we feel calm and secure. Can we feel peaceful even when we are in the middle of a problem? Yes, we can! Peace carries with it the idea of unity, completeness, rest, ease, and security. The prophet Isaiah said God keeps us in perfect peace when we are thinking about Him. When trouble and problems come, sometimes all we can think about is how hard things are. But we must choose to turn our thoughts away from the problems and focus our minds on God.

When our minds are on God, we won't be worried about the future, because we know it is in His hands. We won't get upset about what *might* happen, because our lives are built upon the solid rock of Christ Jesus.

When we yield to worry, we deny our Guide the right to lead us forward in His all-loving care.

WITNESS TO THE WORLD

Rejoice with those who rejoice, and weep with those who weep.
ROMANS 12:15

If you add food coloring to water and then put the stems of white flowers in the water, what happens? Well, if you leave the flowers there about eight hours in the daytime, they'll turn the color of the water! As the water in the flowers evaporates, the stems "drink up" the colored water, and the flowers change color.

This little science experiment is a good example of why Christians need to be careful about how we live among people who don't know Jesus yet.

Nearly everyone Jesus spent time with was an outcast—someone most people treated in an unfriendly way. But His relationship with them was not just about friendship. He wanted to bring them back to God.

Like Jesus, we are to be in the world, but not of the world. When you donate to a toy drive for sick children, you are *in* the world, showing that you care. But if you start using swear words like some of the players on your team, then you are *of* the world, becoming like those players instead of letting them see Jesus in you. Are you loving people in the world without being changed by them?

DISCOVER GOD'S GRACE

We have depended on God's grace.
2 CORINTHIANS 1:12 NLT

When you sit down in a chair, you depend on it to hold you up. When it's dinnertime, you depend on your mom or dad to provide the food you need to eat. Depending on objects or people means counting on them to do what they are supposed to do.

Can we depend on God to guide and help us every day, and especially when we face a problem?

Yes! God has promised to give us His guidance and help, and He always keeps His promises. But to be honest, sometimes it's hard for us to rely on God instead of ourselves. Sometimes we think we have to face a problem or make a hard decision all by ourselves. We don't even think to ask God for His advice and help!

Put God to the test when troubles come. He won't let you down. In the midst of a painful illness, the apostle Paul begged God to take it away. But God replied, "My grace is enough for you" (2 Corinthians 12:9 ICB). You can always depend on God's strength and help when troubles come. Just like Paul trusted God no matter what, you can too.

A HOME IN HEAVEN

"If I go and prepare a place for you, I will come
again and receive you to Myself."

JOHN 14:3

Have you ever thought about what Heaven will be like? One summer night a father took his children on a walk. Looking up at the stars, his young daughter exclaimed, "Daddy, if this side of Heaven is so beautiful, the other side must really be amazing!"

When Jesus was on earth, He didn't have His own home. He once said, "Foxes have holes and birds of the air have nests, but the Son of Man has no place to lay his head" (Matthew 8:20 NIV). How different from the home in Heaven He left in order to come to earth! The Bible tells us Heaven is filled with more wonders and glory than we can imagine. Why did Jesus give up His amazing home? Because of His love for you and me.

But the story doesn't end there. Now Jesus has returned to Heaven—and someday we will join Him! Think of it: He wants to share Heaven's glory with us!

SAFE AND SECURE

Those who live in the shelter of the Most High will
find rest in the shadow of the Almighty.
PSALM 91:1 NLT

Have you ever looked into a kaleidoscope? When you turn the end of the tube as you look inside, what do you see? Beautiful, colorful, always-changing patterns!

Life can be full of changes. Even good things that happen—like moving to a new house, the birth of a little brother or sister, or winning a school election—often involve change. Sometimes we wish that things could stay the same! Someone has said that the only certainty in life is uncertainty.

Deep inside all of us is a longing for security—it's a longing that will not go away. We know we need a solid foundation for our lives. Where can we find it?

King David knew the answer. He said, "Those who live in the shelter of the Most High will find rest in the shadow of the Almighty." Only God never changes. His love does not change, and neither do His promises. That is why we can look to Him for security and stability, even when our lives are changing. Is your security in Jesus?

FILLED WITH GOD'S LOVE

"Love one another as I have loved you."
JOHN 15:12

Preschoolers learn that up is the opposite of down, and under is the opposite of over. Fast is the opposite of slow. Day is the opposite of night.

What is the opposite of love?

Well, think about this. To love others means to do what is best for them. So if we choose not to do something good for others because we'd rather spend the time or money on ourselves, we aren't loving them. We're being selfish. The opposite of love isn't hate. The opposite of love is selfishness.

St. Francis of Assisi learned that being concerned about others and doing things to help them is the way to be happy. Here is part of his now-famous prayer: "Grant that I may not so much seek to be consoled as to console, to be understood as to understand, to be loved as to love. For it is in giving that we receive. It is in pardoning that we are pardoned. It is in dying that we are born to eternal life."

Do you want to be happy? Ask the Holy Spirit to help you be unselfish and fill you with His love.

MAY 23

A POSITIVE INFLUENCE

Do not be conformed to this world, but be transformed.
ROMANS 12:2

Every day our actions show others if we are becoming more like Jesus.

If our actions show that we are living for God, we will treat other people like we would want to be treated. They will see the difference Jesus makes in our lives. But we don't want to do the same things as people who don't know Jesus—gossip, lie, steal, bully, or disobey our parents. If we do those things, others won't see Jesus in our lives and won't want to know more about Him.

We might need to make some changes if we want to show Jesus to others with our lives. We will need to stop doing things the world says are right and start doing the things God says are right. We will need to be *transformed*. We can't do this by ourselves, but with the help of the Holy Spirit, we can! As we keep praying and reading and obeying God's Word, the Holy Spirit will help us become more like Jesus and obey the Bible's clear command: "Do not be conformed to this world."

So don't let the world change you—let God change you! Then you will be a positive influence for Jesus in everything you do.

YOU CAN CHOOSE

I have set before you life and death . . . ; therefore choose life.
DEUTERONOMY 30:19

*D*rones and robotic technologies, like artificial arms, can do more and more things that only humans used to do. But there's one thing robots will never be able to do—make their own choices.

When God created us, He gave us the ability to choose. If God made us so we could only do good things and never do anything wrong, we would be like robots. We wouldn't be able to *choose* to do good instead of evil.

And if we couldn't make choices, we also couldn't love. Robots do not love! God created us with the capacity to love. True love is a choice. We can't force anyone to love us or be our friend. And God won't force us to choose loving actions toward others either. He wants us to be free to choose.

It might be fun to be a robot for a day. But I would rather be able to make choices and be responsible for my actions than be a robot for very long! Are you using your ability to make choices wisely—and using it for God?

HOW TO STOP SINNING

In all these things we are more than conquerors
through Him who loved us.
ROMANS 8:37

You might have heard someone joke, "The Devil made me do it." But the truth is that Satan, the Devil, can't *make* us do anything. He does attack us and try to get us to sin, but Christians are not his prisoners of war. We don't have to live in defeat, unable to stop sinning. As we grow in Jesus, we can live with more and more victory over sin.

Are you tempted to lie, cheat, or steal? Are you sometimes unkind to other kids? Do you sometimes disobey your parents? With Jesus' help, you can stop doing these things.

There is only one way to have that victory, though. It's by walking closely with Jesus every day. Tell Him when you are tempted, and ask for His help not to sin. The closer we are to Jesus, the farther we are from Satan!

The Bible says, "Resist the devil and he will flee from you. Draw near to God and He will draw near to you" (James 4:7—8). Is the Devil farther away from you today than he was a week ago?

GIVE GOD CONTROL

This is God, our God forever and ever; He will be our guide even to death.

PSALM 48:14

There is a story about a little girl whose father was an airline pilot. On one of his flights across the ocean, the pilot took his daughter with him. As the plane flew over the Atlantic at night, a storm came up. The little girl had fallen asleep, but a flight attendant woke her and told her to fasten her seat belt because of the bad weather. The girl saw all the lightning flashing around the plane.

"Is Daddy at the controls?" she asked.

The flight attendant replied, "Yes, your father is in the cockpit."

The little girl smiled, closed her eyes, and went back to sleep.

God wants to be at the controls of our lives, but He gives us the freedom to be in control if we wish. The problem is that we would crash if we took the controls of an airplane we had not been taught to fly.

God knows everything about us. He loves us, and He knows what is best for us. If we will let Him have the controls, He will see us safely through every day.

MAY 27

PRAISE GOD ALWAYS

[God] gives us the victory through our Lord Jesus Christ.
1 CORINTHIANS 15:57 NIV

It's easy to sing praise songs when the sun is shining and our lives are going well. It can be harder to praise God when we're feeling down.

There was a time when Martin Luther, the German church reformer of the sixteenth century, felt discouraged for a while. His sad face and attitude day after day were affecting his whole family. Then one day his wife came to the breakfast table all dressed in black, as if she were going to a funeral. Luther asked, "Who died?"

She replied, "Martin, the way you've been behaving lately, I thought God had died, so I came prepared to attend His funeral." What she was really telling him was that he'd been choosing to be sad when he had reasons to be happy. Luther understood her point. He decided that he wouldn't allow worry, resentment, discouragement, or frustration to defeat him. Instead, he would trust the Savior and have joy about God's grace, no matter what happened.

Have you ever praised God when you were feeling sad? Don't wait until you "feel like it," or you'll never do it. Instead, praise Him first, and then you'll feel like it!

ONE WAY

"I am the way, the truth, and the life. No one
comes to the Father except through Me."

JOHN 14:6

Does your family like to take road trips to places you've never been before? Maybe you've traveled to the Grand Canyon, Mount Rushmore, or Niagara Falls. The only sure way to reach your destination was to use your GPS or a good road map or to ask someone who knew the way. Not just any road would take you where you wanted to go.

Some people say all roads lead to God. They mean that any religion or faith will get you to Heaven. But that's not true. The reason? There is a roadblock that keeps us from reaching God—the roadblock of sin. But God has provided a map—the Bible—and He has provided the One who knows the way and can give us directions—Jesus.

Jesus didn't say, "I am one of many ways to God." He said, "I am the way." He wasn't bragging or lacking compassion when He said that. It was the truth. Only Jesus came from Heaven to pay the price for our sins. If we follow Him, we will never be lost!

DISCIPLINE FOR SUCCESS

Be wise. . . . Use your time in the best way you can.
COLOSSIANS 4:5 ICB

All athletes know they must work hard to do well in their sport. Even the most talented athletes require a routine that includes conditioning, strength training, skill drills, and hours of practice, practice, practice.

Legendary football coach Vince Lombardi said, "The only place success comes before work is in the dictionary." The same kind of discipline is needed in any field. Before you can expect success, honor, or applause, you will need to put in time to learn what you need to know.

The master musician knows that months of practice and self-sacrifice come before a perfect performance. The student knows that years of study, self-denial, and commitment precede the triumphant day of graduation with honors. Astronauts spend years training for a flight that can be as short as a few days.

The Bible teaches that sacrifice and discipline are necessary if we want to be faithful servants of Jesus. The apostle Paul wrote, "I discipline my body like an athlete, training it to do what it should" (1 Corinthians 9:27 NLT).

How will you discipline your time . . . your eyes . . . your mind . . . your body today for the sake of Jesus?

HOPE FOR THE HOME

He lifted the poor out of their suffering. And he made
their families grow like flocks of sheep.

PSALM 107:41 ICB

A picture is worth a thousand words." This famous saying means that the right picture can help us understand what it's like to be in a particular place. A beautiful picture of Yosemite National Park can help us think about what it's like to stand under giant sequoia trees.

When a man and a woman get married, God wants their relationship to be a picture of the relationship between Jesus and His church. The way a husband and wife love each other should help people understand how much Jesus loves His followers and how much they love Him.

God gave marriage to us, and His standards have not changed. Jesus said, "A man shall leave his father and mother and be joined to his wife. . . . Therefore what God has joined together, let not man separate" (Matthew 19:5–6).

If divorce has happened in your family, God can forgive the past, heal the present, and give hope for the future. Remember that children are never responsible for divorce. And decide now that when you marry, you'll treasure your spouse as a gift from God and work to make your marriage a picture of God's love.

MAY 31

JESUS WILL ANSWER

He will give his angels charge of you to guard you in all your ways.
PSALM 91:11 RSV

I n China, a woman walked through the foothills with her baby in a carrier on her back and her little child right beside her. Just as they reached the top of a hill, they heard a roar. The woman turned and saw a tiger springing at her, followed by two cubs.

The woman had never attended church, but a missionary had told her about Jesus. "He is able to help you when you are in trouble," the missionary had said. As the tiger's claws tore into her arm, the woman cried out, "Oh, Jesus, help me!"

The tiger, instead of attacking again, suddenly turned and ran away with her cubs.

You probably will never be attacked by a wild tiger. But we all are attacked sometimes by other "beasts" like fear, worry, loneliness, or doubt. When that happens, cry out to Jesus, and He will answer you!

JUNE

God is our protection and our strength. He
always helps in times of trouble.

PSALM 46:1 ICB

JESUS' PRECIOUS BLOOD

Jesus Christ . . . loved us and washed us from our sins in His own blood.
REVELATION 1:5

If you have a cavity or a toothache, you wouldn't ask a car mechanic to fix your tooth. If you need help improving your gymnastic skills, you wouldn't ask a football coach for help. There are some things only the right person can do.

Jesus did things that *no one else* could do. He made blind people see and disabled people walk. He walked on water and calmed a storm. He brought dead people back to life.

But what is the most important thing Jesus did that no one else could do? He died for us and paid for our sins.

When J. P. Morgan, the multimillionaire, died, it was found that he left directions for where his money should go. They included his most important request: "I commit my soul into the hands of my Savior, in full confidence that, having redeemed and washed it in His most precious blood, He will present it faultless before my heavenly Father; and I ask my children to follow Jesus." This man knew his great wealth could not save him. No matter who we are or what we have done, only Jesus can save us, for only "the blood of Jesus . . . cleanses us from all sin" (1 John 1:7).

READY TO LISTEN

"Whatever things you ask when you pray, believe that
you receive them, and you will have them."

MARK 11:24

D o you know someone who is a good listener—someone who is always glad to listen to you? Prayer is talking to God about the concerns of our hearts, and God is a very good listener.

More than memorized prayers or just asking God to bless everyone, God wants to hear what you think and feel and care about and need.

The Bible says, "Whatever we ask we receive from Him, because we keep His commandments and do those things that are pleasing in His sight" (1 John 3:22). God loves to hear and answer our prayers when we have hearts that are ready to listen to Him and we love to obey Him.

God delights in the prayers of His children—prayers that express our love for Him, prayers that share our deepest concerns with Him. "Come boldly to the throne of grace, that [you] may obtain mercy and find grace to help in time of need" (Hebrews 4:16). God is ready and waiting to listen to you!

HEAVENLY SAVINGS

"Store your treasures in heaven. . . . Wherever your treasure
is, there the desires of your heart will also be."
MATTHEW 6:20—21 NLT

An old man, a great man of God, was close to death. He told his
grandson, "I don't know what type of work I will be doing in Heaven,
but if it's allowed, I'm going to ask the Lord Jesus to let me help build
your mansion. You be sure you send up plenty of the right materials."

What did the grandfather mean? What kinds of "materials" can be
sent up to Heaven? Loving others, obeying God, sharing our faith, sharing our possessions, doing good wherever we can in Jesus' name—we
can think of all these things as the right materials to send up. All these
things we do out of love for God are so valuable in Heaven, they're con-
sidered treasures there. So the more we do them—because we care
about what God cares about—the more we'll be storing treasures in
Heaven. Or, as the grandfather said, we'll be sending up the right materials for building a mansion in Heaven.

What kinds of materials are you sending up to Heaven?

REST FOR THE WEARY

"Come to Me . . . and I will give you rest."

MATTHEW 11:28

Jesus got tired and needed to sleep just like we do. Sometimes we forget that Jesus was human as well as God. He knew what it meant to work long hours. He had calluses on His hands from all the carpentry work He did. If the chisel slipped and cut His finger, His blood was red and warm, like ours.

This is one of the reasons Jesus could say, "Come to me, all of you who are tired and have heavy loads. I will give you rest" (Matthew 11:28 ICB). Jesus knows what it is to be exhausted after a long day.

But the greatest work Jesus did was not in the carpenter's shop, nor at the marriage feast in Cana where He turned the water into wine. The greatest work Jesus did was not when He made the blind to see, the deaf to hear, the mute to speak, nor even the dead to rise.

What was His greatest work?

His greatest work was what He accomplished through the cross and resurrection. There the burden of our sins was placed on Him, and there He won our salvation. And that is why we can come by faith to Him, and He will give us rest.

WHAT A FRIEND!

God is our protection and our strength. He
always helps in times of trouble.
PSALM 46:1 ICB

Jesus' disciples once tried to stop children from coming close to Jesus, but He said, "Let the little children come to me. Don't stop them, because the kingdom of God belongs to people who are like these little children" (Luke 18:16 ICB). Then He held and blessed the children. Don't you think all those children found a new Friend that day?

Through the years many people have come to know Jesus as their Savior and their Friend—sometimes in the midst of difficult circumstances. "What a Friend We Have in Jesus," a hymn that has been a favorite for nearly two hundred years, came out of the experience of a young man whose bride drowned on the night before their wedding. In his sadness, he turned to Jesus and found a Friend, peace, and comfort. He wrote about how Jesus can bear "all our sins and griefs," and that "He'll take and shield" us in His arms.

Sometimes we face disappointment and sadness. Yet even sorrows turn to blessings when they make us discover that Jesus truly is our faithful Friend!

TAKE THE LEAP

By my God I can leap over a wall.
PSALM 18:29

Extreme sports, like snowboarding and rock climbing, are difficult and risky. Athletes do tricks in midair or climb steep, smooth rock formations and count on their skills to help them survive. They wouldn't be able to take on the challenges of their sport if it weren't for all the time they've spent practicing and all the help they've received from coaches.

In one of his psalms, King David wrote, "By my God I can leap over a wall." We all can jump over some barriers in life by our own efforts. But some "walls" we face are higher and more challenging.

You might have a serious health problem or a disability. You might have a problem with anger or anxiety. Or maybe one of your parents has lost a job. When we try to jump over walls like these by ourselves, we repeatedly fail. But with God's help, we can deal with these situations.

What walls do you need to conquer? A bad habit? An emotion like doubt or fear? An attitude that separates you from others? Whatever it is, with God's help you can leap over that wall.

JUNE 7

SEALED WITH THE SPIRIT

Having believed, you were marked in him with
a seal, the promised Holy Spirit.
EPHESIANS 1:13 NIV

Long ago, kings sent letters and announcements written on parchment and sealed with the king's own special stamp pressed into hot wax. The seal meant that the letter or announcement came with the authority of the king.

God places a seal on us when we receive Jesus. That seal is a person—the Holy Spirit. When an envelope is sealed, whatever is inside has a special purpose and is protected. The *seal* of the Spirit is a sign that we belong to God and are safe with Him.

The Spirit is also God's *pledge*, or promise, to help us through our lives and bring us home to Heaven. And our relationship with the Spirit is a sample of what we can expect when we get there.

Finally, the Spirit *witnesses* to us, or tells us, through the Bible and within our hearts, that Jesus died for us and that we have become God's children.

What a wonderful thing to know that God has given us the Holy Spirit as a seal, a pledge, and a witness!

A CLEAR CONSCIENCE

I myself always strive to have a conscience
without offense toward God and men.
ACTS 24:16

A ship without a rudder will never get to its destination. In fact, without a rudder, a ship has no direction at all and is just tossed and blown about by the wind and waves of the sea. Without our conscience, we would be just like a rudderless ship.

God gives everyone a conscience to guide them. When your actions please God, your conscience tells you that you're going in the right direction. You have peace with God and other people—you don't feel ashamed or worried about being caught or punished for doing something wrong.

When we accept Jesus as our Savior, He forgives all our sin—and that gives us a clear conscience too! But just like a rudder can break down, our conscience can break down too. Over time, continuing to sin can dull our conscience so much that it can't steer our ship—our lives—anymore.

To keep your conscience working right, let God's Word teach and sharpen your conscience every day. God will lead you "in the paths of righteousness for His name's sake" (Psalm 23:3). When you follow God's Word, your conscience will be clear.

What is your conscience telling you today?

JUNE 9

TWO THINGS TO DO

Give your worries to the Lord. He will take care of you.
PSALM 55:22 ICB

This popular little prayer expresses a big and important thought: "God, grant me the serenity to accept the things I cannot change, the courage to change the things I can, and the wisdom to know the difference."

Some things can't be changed, and we must accept them. And some things God wants us *not* to accept, but (with His help) work to change. We need to do both of these—accepting some things and working to change others.

If others at school are being laughed at or bullied because of their disabilities or because they are not good students, that is something you can work to change. You can speak up for them and talk to an adult about other ways to help. But if your best friend moves away or your grandparent dies, you can't change that, as much as you would like to and as sad as you will feel. We have to choose to trust God with everything—that He'll guide us in the things we can do—and to believe He is always good, even in the things we have no control over.

Our heavenly Father wants us to learn to trust Him. "Give your worries to the Lord. He will take care of you."

GOOD PROMISES

Blessed be the LORD. . . . There has not failed
one word of all His good promise.
1 KINGS 8:56

When a man and a woman get married, they exchange rings as symbols of their promises to each other. When people in business promise to work together, they sign a contract. When your parents buy a house or a car, they might have made a down payment, with a promise to pay the rest of the price over time. The rings, the contract, and the down payment are signs and guarantees that we will keep our promises and our word.

God has made some incredible promises to us! He promised that we can have a relationship with Him through His Son. He promised to be with us always and to provide everything we need. He promised to take us to Heaven when we die. The Bible is full of God's promises. He has given His word!

Sometimes people ask, "What guarantee do we have that God's promises can be trusted?" God guarantees His promises with the most precious sign anyone could give—His Son, Jesus, whose death and resurrection purchased our salvation—completely and fully!

GOD HEARS US

"Ask, and you will receive, that your joy may be full."
JOHN 16:24

Just think—you and I have the incredible privilege of talking to the God who made Heaven and earth, the God of the whole universe! And we can tell Him anything we want and ask Him anything. Jesus' death and resurrection opened the way for us to talk with God like children talk with their father.

The Bible says that we should pray, believing in God's promise that when "we ask anything according to His will, He hears us" (1 John 5:14). So we can ask God to help us when we are sick, and we can thank Him for making us well. We can ask Him to help us remember what we studied for our math test and thank Him for helping us learn. We can tell God about our concern for friends who don't know Jesus and praise Him when we get to share the gospel with them.

FULL OF JOY

The fruit of the Spirit is . . . joy.
GALATIANS 5:22

The Bible doesn't say, "Count it all joy when you fall into a comfy chair." It says, "Count it all joy when you fall into various trials" (James 1:2). If someone laughs at you for being a Christian, that's a reason for joy!

Joy is not the same as happiness. Happiness depends on whether we're in a good or bad situation. We are happy when we get birthday gifts. We are happy when we eat our favorite meal. We are happy when we laugh with a friend. When things go our way, we are happy.

But joy depends on God. Happiness can disappear when we have problems. But joy never leaves us. We are joyful because we know God. It doesn't matter if things are going our way or not, we can still be joyful!

Joy comes from knowing this world is only temporary, and someday we will be with God forever. It comes from the fact that although we do not yet see God, we believe in Him. He gives us "a joy that cannot be explained" and "is full of glory" (1 Peter 1:8 ICB).

JUNE 13

THINKING AHEAD

"If I go and prepare a place for you, I will come again."
JOHN 14:3

When you start a big school project, it's good to think ahead. You need to know your goal, the steps to take to finish the project, and the supplies you need. Having a good plan and staying focused on your goal make getting to that goal a lot easier.

As Christians, we are supposed to keep our eyes on Heaven. Someday we will live forever with Jesus there! And in the meantime, He has work for us to do. Christians care about the world we live in now too. We want to help others in need, and we want to tell others about Jesus! Throughout history, the Christians who did the most good for others were those who kept looking to Jesus and remembering how He wants His followers to live. C. S. Lewis, the author of The Chronicles of Narnia, said, "Aim at heaven, and you will get earth thrown in. Aim at earth, and you will get neither."

So think ahead every day, and remember Jesus' promise: "If I go and prepare a place for you, I will come again and receive you to Myself" (John 14:3).

POWER FOR PROBLEMS

I can do all things through Christ who strengthens me.

PHILIPPIANS 4:13

A friend told me of a nonbeliever who came to him in the midst of a troubled day. Knowing my friend was a Christian, the man asked, "If I get born again, will all of my problems go away?"

"No," said my friend, "but you will have the power to deal with them."

God gives us wisdom and courage. He surrounds us with other believers, our brothers and sisters in Jesus, to teach and encourage us.

Satan, the enemy of our souls, will always try to discourage us because we belong to Jesus. When we face a problem, he might even whisper, "See, God doesn't care about you!" But with the Holy Spirit's help, we can fight the evil one and recognize his lies. Whatever problems or troubles you might be facing today, God will provide everything you need to see you through.

JUNE 15

BE FREE

Draw near to God and He will draw near to you.
JAMES 4:8

One day a little boy was playing with a vase. He put his hand into it, and he couldn't pull it out. His father tried his best to get the little boy's hand out, but he couldn't do it either. They were thinking of breaking the vase when the father said, "Now, Son, try one more time. Open your hand, hold your fingers out straight like this, and then pull your hand out."

"Oh no, Daddy," said the little boy. "I couldn't put my fingers out like that, because if I did, I would drop my penny."

Sometimes we are like that little boy. His penny, which wouldn't buy much, meant more to him than getting his hand free of that vase. Sometimes we want to hold on to what *we* think is important rather than have what *God* says is important——freedom from sin.

Is there something keeping you from God today? Are you holding on to something you think is more important than God? Let go, and let God have His way in your life.

GOD GIVES HIS ANGELS

His angels . . . keep you in all your ways.
PSALM 91:11

On a deserted, narrow mountain road along a steep cliff, three missionaries realized they needed to turn their car around and go back down the mountain. But how? They could barely see in the heavy snow, and there wasn't much room—they could easily fall off the cliff. They prayed. A car appeared, coming from the opposite direction. A man stepped out and offered to turn the missionaries' car for them, and then he told the missionaries to follow him down the mountain, which they gladly did. Near the bottom, the man's car suddenly disappeared.

Reports like this can only be explained as heavenly help from God's angels! In the Bible, angels sometimes could be seen—at the birth of Jesus, for example. But usually angels go about their business unseen and unrecognized. They never draw attention to themselves, but point us to Jesus instead.

God has given "His angels charge over you, to keep you in all your ways" (Psalm 91:11). But we don't want to worship them or focus on them. Instead, we should thank God for His angels and be glad for their unseen care!

GOD'S TRUE PURPOSES

"Whatever you ask in My name, that I will do."
JOHN 14:13

Prayer makes us partners with God in what He is doing in the world. God works through our prayers!

Jesus gave us a model prayer to use as a guide when we pray. It ends this way: "Yours is the kingdom and the power and the glory forever" (Matthew 6:13). We must pray for God's glory, not just what we want. And God receives glory when we pray for His will for the world— for people everywhere to come to Jesus and receive His salvation. Our Lord said to His disciples, "Whatever you ask in My name, that I will do, that the Father may be glorified in the Son" (John 14:13).

Prayer links us with God's true purposes, for us and for the world. It not only brings the blessings of God's will to our own personal lives, it brings us the added blessing of being in step with God's plan. Have you prayed to your heavenly Father today?

WHITER THAN SNOW

Wash me, and I shall be whiter than snow.

PSALM 51:7

Snow is so white that one can see almost anything that is dropped on it, even at great distances. Take the whitest object you can find—like a brand-new T-shirt—and put it next to snow, and it will look dingy by comparison.

Our lives are like that. If you compare yourself to some other kids you know, you may think you are quite a good person! But compared to God's purity, all of us look dingy and dirty, like a clean T-shirt looks compared to snow.

The good news is that in spite of our sins, God still loves us. And because He loves us, He decided to provide a purity and goodness for us that we could never have on our own. That is why He gave His Son, Jesus, to die for us on the cross. Only when our sins have been washed away—because we've put our faith in Jesus—will we be even whiter than snow to God.

Thank God today that you are now "whiter than snow," because "you were washed . . . in the name of the Lord Jesus and by the Spirit of our God" (1 Corinthians 6:11)!

BE A FRUIT TREE

The fruit of the Spirit is love, joy, peace, . . . gentleness, self-control.
GALATIANS 5:22–23

I f you were a fruit tree, what kind would you be? An apple tree? An orange tree? Or something else? Did you know that all Christians are supposed to produce fruit? But not fruit to eat! Instead, we should produce the fruit of the Spirit in our lives. Or to put it more accurately, we should allow the Holy Spirit to produce His fruit in our lives.

What is the fruit of the Spirit? Galatians 5:22–23 tells us: "love, joy, peace, patience, kindness, goodness, faithfulness, gentleness, self-control" (ICB).

We can't produce this fruit on our own, but when the Spirit of God lives inside us, He will make the fruit grow. Our job is to give Him control so He can work. I might have an apple tree in my yard, but if the soil isn't enriched and the bugs aren't controlled, it won't grow many apples. What might be keeping the Holy Spirit from producing His fruit in your life?

LIKE A MIST

What is your life? You are a mist that appears
for a little while and then vanishes.

JAMES 4:14 NIV

Several years ago a university student asked me what had been my biggest surprise in life. Immediately I replied, "The shortness of life." Young people usually don't think about this, but as people get older, they begin to realize that it is true. Almost before we know it, the years have passed and life is almost over.

If ever we are to live for Jesus and share Him with others, it must be now. Jesus said, "The night is coming when no one can work" (John 9:4).

But knowing that life is short should also comfort us. Before long, we'll be in Heaven! Whenever trouble comes, we know it will soon be over. The apostle Paul wrote, "We have small troubles for a while now, but they are helping us gain an eternal glory. That glory is much greater than the troubles. . . . What we see will last only a short time" (2 Corinthians 4:17–18 ICB).

Enjoy every day of your life. Don't live as if this life will continue forever. It won't. Live instead looking forward to Heaven!

FREE BUT NOT CHEAP

"If anyone desires to come after Me, let him . . .
take up his cross, and follow Me."
MATTHEW 16:24

In the twentieth century, a man named Bill Borden walked away from his family fortune to become a missionary to China. He only got as far as Egypt when he died of typhoid fever. But before he died, he said that he had no regrets!

Another missionary named Jim Elliott, who also lost his life while in ministry, is known for saying, "He is no fool who gives what he cannot keep to gain that which he cannot lose." These men gave their lives on earth, but gained life forever with Jesus.

Following Jesus is always costly. No, it may not cost us our lives. But it will cost us our plans and our selfish desires. Jesus said, "If anyone desires to come after Me, let him deny himself, and take up his cross, and follow Me" (Matthew 16:24). This means we turn our lives over to Jesus as Lord.

Someone has said, "Salvation is free, but not cheap." It cost Jesus His life, and it will cost us too. But nothing could be greater or more satisfying. Follow Jesus, and at the end of your life you will be able to say, "I have no regrets!"

WONDERFUL HELPER

"He is the Spirit of truth who comes from the
Father. . . . He will tell about me."
JOHN 15:26 ICB

Sometimes people call God's Spirit "the Holy Ghost." But the Spirit is not a ghost, and ghosts aren't even real!

God the Holy Spirit is equal with God the Father and God the Son in every way. We call God the Father, Son, and Holy Spirit the *Trinity*, which means "three in one." Although it is difficult for us to understand, God is one God in three Persons—Father, Son, and Holy Spirit.

The Bible also teaches that the Holy Spirit is a Person. He is never to be called "it." He is not an unknowable power or force. He is a mighty Person, the Holy Spirit of God.

The Bible tells us that the Spirit is *omnipotent* and *omnipresent*. Those big words mean that He has all power and that He is everywhere at the same time.

What does this mean for us? In the Bible the Holy Spirit is also called the Comforter and the Helper. What a wonderful Helper to have with us every moment of every day!

ALL WE NEED

"My grace is all you need."
2 CORINTHIANS 12:9 NLT

H ave you ever done something hard that you *really* didn't want to do, but you knew you had to? Maybe you had to get some shots at a doctor's appointment or move away from your best friend because a parent got a new job.

Nothing we do will compare with how hard it was for Jesus to die on the cross for our sins. Right before He went to the cross, Jesus prayed perhaps the greatest, most moving prayer ever uttered. In it, our Lord asked that He would not have to be crucified. But then He said, "Yet I want your will to be done, not mine" (Matthew 26:39 NLT). What strength and courage!

The apostle Paul followed Jesus' example. Paul asked God to take away a painful problem—pain in his body. But God did not take it away. Instead, he told Paul, "My grace is all you need." Rather than complain or become angry, Paul gladly accepted God's will. He discovered that God's help and strength truly were all he needed.

Jesus wants to be with you in any trouble you might have. Call upon His name. He might not make your problem go away, but He will give you His help and strength.

CHANGED

We are being changed to be like him.

2 CORINTHIANS 3:18 ICB

Pigs love mud. You can scrub a pig, spray the best perfume on him, put a ribbon around his neck, and bring him in the house. But when you turn him loose, he will jump into the first mud puddle he sees because his nature has not changed. He is still a pig!

Do you try to be the best you that you can be? You might decide to work harder on a school subject that's difficult for you or do your chores at home without complaining. These are good decisions and good changes to make.

But God says we all need another change as well—a transformation of the heart. And it is possible! When we come to Jesus, God's Spirit comes to live inside us and change us. Our attitudes, goals, and habits change.

These changes don't happen all at once. We will spend the rest of our lives learning what it means to follow Jesus. But it begins now, as we open our hearts to Him. Are you "being changed to be like him"?

MAKING GOOD DECISIONS

Then the king . . . rejected the advice of the elders.
2 CHRONICLES 10:13

How many decisions will you make today? How many of those will be big, important decisions? Sometimes we think our small decisions don't matter, but all decisions have consequences. If you decided to eat nothing but junk food, eventually you would lose your health. Bad decisions always result in bad consequences.

The Bible warns us, "A person harvests only what he plants" (Galatians 6:7 ICB). In the Old Testament, King Rehoboam stubbornly rejected wise advice and listened only to those who agreed with what he wanted to do. That caused conflict, and the nation of Israel split into two kingdoms.

Life is filled with decisions—many small ones, but some life changing. How will you make them? The most important thing I can tell you is this: Seek God's will in every decision. Pray. Turn to the Bible. Listen to the advice of your Christian friends. Ask the Holy Spirit to guide you. God loves you, and His way is always best.

WHAT GOD CALLS WISDOM

> He Himself is our peace, who . . . has broken
> down the middle wall of separation.
>
> EPHESIANS 2:14

Some time ago a university professor was quoted as saying, "There are two things that will never be solved—the problems of race and war." Perhaps he was right. The Bible shows us that both racism and war begin in the pride and selfishness of the human heart. Until hearts are changed, people everywhere in the world fall back into the same ugly sins.

What can we do about this? What can you do? The Bible calls Jesus the "Prince of Peace" (Isaiah 9:6). He shattered the prejudices of His day by reaching out to those of another race, and He expects us to do the same.

Jesus died not only to give us forgiveness for our sins but also to give each of us a changed life. Ask God to help you share His love with those around you.

JUNE 27

TRUST AND OBEY

Blessed is the man who makes the Lord his trust.
PSALM 40:4 NIV

Some years ago someone gave my young son a dollar. My son brought me the dollar bill and said, "Daddy, keep this for me." But in a few minutes he came back and said, "Daddy, I'd better keep my own dollar." He tucked it in his pocket and went out to play. In a few minutes he came back with tears in his eyes and said, "Daddy, I lost my dollar. Help me find it!"

How often do we give our concerns and problems to the Lord and then take matters back into our own hands? We are like my son giving me his dollar for safekeeping but taking it back again. We try to solve everything ourselves, and then when we have messed things up, we pray, "Oh, Lord, help me! I'm in trouble!"

We always have a choice. Do you want to put your life safely in God's "pocket" or keep it in your own? The Bible's promise is true: "Blessed is the man who makes the Lord his trust."

WHAT A CHANGE!

He made Him . . . to be sin for us, that we might
become the righteousness of God in Him.

2 CORINTHIANS 5:21

Have you ever made a crayon rubbing? Place a sheet of paper over a leaf, and then color over the leaf. The shape of the leaf will appear on the page. It *transfers* from the leaf to the paper.

The Bible tells us about the most important transfer ever. On the cross, the sins of all people were transferred to Jesus. And when we come to Jesus, God transfers Jesus' righteousness—His sinlessness—to us. Once we were sinners in God's eyes; now He sees us as righteous because of Jesus.

How could this happen? The Bible says, "No one is righteous—not even one" (Romans 3:10 NLT). But when we accept Jesus, it's like we change clothes. We get to wear the white robe of Jesus' righteousness instead of the rags of our sin. Our sins were transferred to Him—and His righteousness is transferred to us!

Did we deserve it? No. Did we earn it? No. It is all because of God's grace. We can never win God's approval by anything we do, no matter how good we are. Only Jesus can save us. Let's thank God for transferring our bad actions to Jesus and Jesus' righteousness to us!

PEACE, PERFECT PEACE

I will give you assured peace in this place.
JEREMIAH 14:13

Someone once said that worry is like sitting in a rocking chair—it gives you something to do, but it doesn't get you anywhere.

God doesn't want you to worry. He is your heavenly Father who loves you and cares for you. The next time you start to worry, think about this. Imagine a fierce ocean storm beating against a rocky shore. The lightning flashes, the thunder roars, and the waves crash over the rocks. But then you see a crack in the rocky cliff—and inside is a little bird fast asleep, its head snugly tucked under its wing. The bird knows the rock will protect it, and so it sleeps in peace.

Israel's King David wrote, "The Lord is my rock and my fortress and my deliverer; my God, my strength, in whom I will trust" (Psalm 18:2). We can say the same thing. Jesus is our Rock, and we are secure with Him forever, no matter what happens around us. Like little birds in a storm, we can rest as we trust in Him.

KEEP HEAVEN IN VIEW

We are hard-pressed on every side, yet not crushed.

2 CORINTHIANS 4:8

Have you ever seen a searchlight? It's like a giant flashlight that shines up into the night sky to bring people's attention to something new and exciting going on—maybe a concert or the state fair. If you follow the light, you'll arrive at the event.

As Christians we want to keep a bright light shining to help other people arrive in Heaven. I have found in my travels around the world that people who keep Heaven in mind stay calm and cheerful even during days of trouble. When Heaven is more real to us, we aren't easily upset by the problems of life on earth.

Our faith in the future should make us more responsible today. All around us are people who never think about God or Heaven. How will they learn about the future God has prepared for us if we don't tell them about it now, in the present?

JULY

"In the world you will have tribulation; but be of
good cheer, I have overcome the world."
JOHN 16:33

JULY 1

A CLEAN SLATE

Create in me a clean heart, O God, and renew a steadfast spirit within me.
PSALM 51:10

Have you ever seen a big whiteboard after it's been cleaned? When all the board has been wiped off, it's as if nothing at all had ever been written on it.

This is what God does for us when we come to Him, confessing our sin and trusting Jesus as our Savior and Lord. First John 1:9 says, "If we confess our sins, He is faithful and just to forgive us our sins and to cleanse us from all unrighteousness." What does God promise to do? Forgive and cleanse. Our lives are wiped clean! Only God can do that. We can't do it ourselves.

Have you ever wished you could start a day all over again? Let God wipe your life clean—confess your sins to Him, and He will give you a brand-new start!

NO ROOM FOR THE WORLD

The wisdom of this world is foolishness with God.
1 CORINTHIANS 3:19

Sometimes after a big meal, we're so full we don't want to eat even one more bite. There's just no room! In the same way, when our lives are filled with Jesus, there's no room for the things of the world.

God wants us to live *in* the world. He doesn't want us to avoid people who need to hear about Jesus. When He was praying for His disciples, Jesus said, "As You sent Me into the world, I also have sent them into the world" (John 17:18). We can't love people and tell them about Jesus if we stay away from them.

But does God want us to become *like* the world? No. We are to be different. We follow Jesus. What the world says is good and wise, God says is foolish. The Bible says, "These are the evil things in the world: wanting things to please our sinful selves, wanting the sinful things we see, being too proud of the things we have. But none of those things comes from the Father. All of them come from the world" (1 John 2:16 ICB).

Let Jesus fill your life, and there won't be room for the world.

THE LIGHT OF SALVATION

If anyone acknowledges that Jesus is the Son of God, God lives in him.
1 JOHN 4:15 NIV

In a nighttime thunderstorm, rain clouds block the moon and stars—everything is dark. When a flash of lightning strikes, it lights up the whole sky!

Jesus' death on the cross was like a bright light shining into the darkness of sin.

Sin cost God His very best—the life of His Son, Jesus. The angels in Heaven hid their faces and were silent as Jesus died. They couldn't understand God's plan. They wondered why Jesus had to bear the sins of all the world.

But soon they uncovered their faces and began to praise God again. Jesus' death and resurrection defeated Satan. "The light of the gospel of the glory of Christ, who is the image of God" (2 Corinthians 4:4), shattered the terrible darkness of sin.

When we come to Jesus, God's love and light fill our hearts. Is that light shining through you to others?

THE STATUE OF LIBERTY AND THE CROSS

"If the Son makes you free, you shall be free indeed."
JOHN 8:36

The Statue of Liberty in New York Harbor has greeted immigrants to the United States since 1886. Many of the newcomers have arrived with nothing but the clothes they were wearing! They valued freedom more highly than everything they had left behind. They did not take freedom for granted—and neither must we.

The experience of those immigrants is a picture of what we do when we come to Jesus. We decide to leave sin behind, we turn from belonging to this world, and we become citizens of a new kingdom—the kingdom of God. In God's kingdom the "statue of liberty" is the cross!

The statue in New York Harbor shines her lamp for people coming into America. But the cross of Jesus lights our way into a life with God in Heaven!

GOD'S WONDERFUL KNOWLEDGE

Oh, the depth of the riches both of the wisdom and knowledge of God!
ROMANS 11:33

You've probably heard the story about Benjamin Franklin attaching a key to the tail of a kite during a thunderstorm. Why is it said that he did this? He was trying to figure out how electricity worked. People have always tried to understand the world around them. Some facts that were mysteries in the past are recognized now, like the fact that many illnesses are caused by germs. Other mysteries still puzzle us, like whether there is life on Mars. But no matter how much we learn, we can't fully understand all the mysteries of God's creation.

God knows so much more than we do, so putting our faith and trust in Him is right. The next time you look into the night sky, remember these words: "The heavens declare the glory of God" (Psalm 19:1). We know that God created the stars and planets, and He understands all their movements. In fact, He is guiding them, just as surely as He is guiding us!

A GLORIOUS GRANDSTAND

Since we are surrounded by so great a cloud of
witnesses, let us lay aside every . . . sin.
HEBREWS 12:1

Have you ever been inside a huge football stadium, packed with
people, or seen one on TV? The roars and cheers of the crowd help
the competing teams play their best.

An even bigger "heavenly grandstand" is filled with a crowd of
people too. The Bible calls them "a great cloud of witnesses." They are
the people who have gone ahead of us to Heaven. They encourage us
and remind us to keep our faith in Jesus. The angels who rejoice over
sinners who turn to Jesus in faith (Luke 15:10) are there too.

Our God sees everything happening in our lives. The Bible says, "All
things are . . . open to the eyes of Him to whom we must give account"
(Hebrews 4:13). So even if no one else on earth sees you walk away from
gossip, or tell the truth, or give your whole allowance to a missionary,
you actually have a very large audience in Heaven, cheering you on!

JULY 7

THIS IS THE DAY

Put on the armor of light.
ROMANS 13:12 NASB

D o you have an alarm clock to wake you up in the morning? Have you ever hit the snooze button too many times and been late for school or church? I once read about an old clock with this message written on it: "It is later than you think." Whoever made that clock wanted to remind others how short and uncertain life can be.

We Christians have a special kind of "clock" in the Word of God. From beginning to end, it warns us, "It is later than you think." Writing to the Christians of his day, the apostle Paul said, "It is already the hour for you to awaken from sleep; for now salvation is nearer to us than when we believed. The night is almost gone, and the day is at hand. Let us therefore lay aside the deeds of darkness and put on the armor of light" (Romans 13:11–12 NASB).

If you had only one more day to live, how would you spend it? Learn to live each day trusting Jesus, wearing His armor of light, and doing what He says to do.

GOD FEELS WHAT WE FEEL

Through the LORD's mercies we are not consumed,
because His compassions fail not.

LAMENTATIONS 3:22

When I was a boy, I thought of God as an old man with a long white beard. After all, hadn't great artists like Michelangelo painted Him that way? Perhaps I thought God was like an old man in other ways too—somewhat weak and harmless, not really in touch with me and my problems.

Later, as I read the Bible, I realized that God is a spirit. He doesn't have a body, so He isn't confined to one place at a time. But God also is a person: He thinks, He speaks, He loves, He becomes sad or angry. Because God is a person, He understands our feelings.

No matter what your day is like, God understands, and He cares. He even understands our temptations, for His Son, Jesus, was "tempted in every way, just as we are—yet . . . without sin" (Hebrews 4:15 NIV). God's compassion is why you can talk with Him about *anything*, knowing for certain that He will understand!

JULY 9

HUNTING FOR HAPPINESS

"Blessed are those who hunger and thirst for righteousness."
MATTHEW 5:6

Have you ever been on a treasure hunt? Maybe it was part of the fun at a birthday party or an event at church. But what if you were disappointed by the "treasure" you found? Then the hunt didn't seem so much fun after all.

Life can be like this too. We hunt for what we think will make us happy. But the newest video game, fashion trend, or starting spot on the team won't make us happy for long. God is the only Source of true happiness. Only God can give us contentment, security, peace, and hope for the future.

How hard it is for us to believe this! It is understandable if we haven't given our lives to Christ; then, the Bible says, our spiritual "eyes" are still blinded, unable to see God's truth until the Holy Spirit opens them.

That is why the Lord Jesus, in His Sermon on the Mount, said, "Blessed are those who hunger and thirst for righteousness, for they shall be filled" (Matthew 5:6). *Righteousness* means living life God's way. This is God's promise—and it is true.

Make righteousness your goal, and you will find true happiness.

PEACEMAKERS

"Blessed are the peacemakers, for they shall be called sons of God."

MATTHEW 5:9

A battery has a positive end, marked by a plus sign, and a negative end, marked with a minus sign. If you don't put the correct end into a flashlight first, the battery will provide no power. Both the positive and negative connections must be made.

Our faith is like a battery. To have power, we must love God *and* people. Jesus said that we must love the Lord with all our hearts and love our neighbors as ourselves. Our personal faith in God is useless unless we also love people and do good to them.

If we belong to Jesus, we have peace *with* God and the peace *of* God. Then when we show love for others, we become peacemakers. We will live peacefully with our neighbors, and we will lead them to the Source of true peace——Jesus.

Let the peace of Jesus in your life overflow to others today.

I AM THE TRUTH

"You shall know the truth, and the truth shall make you free."
JOHN 8:32

Many today say there is no such thing as absolute truth. Maybe you have heard your favorite singer say that truth is whatever we want it to be. Maybe a friend has said that what is true for you isn't necessarily true for anyone else.

But God's Word makes it clear that this is wrong. Jesus said, "I am the way, the truth, and the life" (John 14:6). Dozens of times He declared, "I tell you the truth." The Bible tells us that "grace and truth came through Jesus Christ" (John 1:17) and that God "chose to give us birth through the word of truth" (James 1:18 NIV).

Let God help you make decisions about what is right and what is wrong. That's the way to live in freedom from sin. God has shown His truth to us in His written Word, the Bible, and in the living Word, Jesus. And because Jesus is Absolute Truth, we can depend on Him absolutely!

FROM DEATH TO LIFE

Even when we were dead in trespasses, [God] made us alive
together with Christ (by grace you have been saved).

EPHESIANS 2:5

Reading his local newspaper, a man glanced at the obituary column. To his surprise he saw his own name, indicating that he had just died. At first he laughed about it. But soon his phone began to ring. Shocked friends and acquaintances were calling his family to offer their sympathy.

The man finally called the newspaper editor and said that even though he had been reported dead in the obituary column, he was very much alive. The embarrassed editor apologized. Then in a flash of inspiration, he said, "Don't worry, sir, I'll make it all right. Tomorrow I'll put your name in the births column!"

This funny incident is also a spiritual lesson. Our names could have appeared in the obituary column one day and in the births column the next. The Bible is marvelously true: "You He made alive, who were dead in trespasses and sins" (Ephesians 2:1). Why did God do this amazing thing for us? Because His "mercy is great, and he loved us very much" (Ephesians 2:4 ICB)!

SPIRITUAL TRAINING

"I will never leave you nor forsake you."
HEBREWS 13:5

Have you ever been bullied, or do you know someone who has? Learning how to deal with a bully is wise. Satan is the ultimate bully, and God wants to teach us how to defend ourselves against him.

Satan will do everything he can to discourage and defeat us. He attacks us where we are weakest. He wants to keep us from serving God and living in Heaven forever.

God offers spiritual training to build us up in our hearts and minds, like physical exercise makes our muscles stronger. He also has given us everything we need to defend ourselves from Satan's attacks. These include reading the Bible, being constant in our faith, and listening to the Holy Spirit, who lives inside us.

God has promised to be with us when we face any trouble. We must remember that He's bigger than every problem and use the weapons He has given us! Most of all, we must never forget that because of Jesus' death and resurrection, Satan has already been defeated—and someday the war will be over.

BEYOND THE STARRY SKY

> We are looking for the city that is to come.
>
> HEBREWS 13:14 NRSV

The apostle Paul wasn't afraid to die. For him, death was the joyful gateway to new life—the life of Heaven. He said, "I long to go and be with Christ" (Philippians 1:23 NLT).

Without the resurrection of Christ, there could be no hope for the future. The Bible promises that someday we are going to stand face-to-face with our living Savior. All our questions will be answered, and all our fears and sadness will disappear.

An old gospel hymn says it well:

> *Face to face with Christ my Savior,*
> *Face to face, what will it be?*
> *When with rapture I behold Him,*
> *Jesus Christ who died for me?*
> *Face to face I shall behold Him,*
> *Far beyond the starry sky;*
> *Face to face in all His glory*
> *I shall see Him by and by.*

—CARRIE E. BRECK

THE BLESSING OF BURDENS

The LORD has comforted his people, and will have
compassion on his suffering ones.
ISAIAH 49:13 NRSV

Our oldest daughter's husband was from Switzerland, and they often spent their summers there. Sometimes we visited them and soared above the countryside on chairlifts high in the Alps. Looking down we could see almost a carpet of wildflowers, some of the most beautiful in the world.

Only a few months earlier, those plants were buried under heavy snow. That snow gave them water and kept them safe from the winter winds. It prepared the wildflowers to grow when spring came. Our burdens can be like that snow, preparing the way for something beautiful once the winter is past.

Comfort and wealth have never enriched the world as much as hardship. Out of pain and trouble have come the sweetest songs, the best poems, the most gripping stories, and the most inspiring lives. Our problems can be like heavy snow in the Alps, making way for something beautiful. God will see to it!

ONLY ONE WAY

Whoever desires, let him take the water of life freely.

REVELATION 22:17

A driver stopped to ask a man on the sidewalk how to get to a certain street. The man gave the driver clear directions, but the driver still asked doubtfully, "Is that the best way?" The man replied, "That is the only way."

There is only one way of salvation, and it is through Jesus. "No one comes to the Father except through Me," Jesus said (John 14:6). Later the apostle Peter told a crowd, "There is no other name under heaven given among men by which we must be saved" (Acts 4:12).

We can receive God's free gift of salvation only one way: by believing in His Son. Only Jesus died for our sins, and only Jesus rose from the dead.

God still offers forgiveness and new life. If you have never done it, turn to Jesus today. And if you do know Him, pray today for someone you know and ask God to help you tell that person the good news about Jesus.

COMMITTED LOVE

Love the LORD your God, . . . walk in all His ways, . . . hold fast to Him.
DEUTERONOMY 11:22

Do you like riding roller coasters? Maybe you felt brave and excited about riding one, but when it was your turn to step into the car, you suddenly felt scared. Then, instead of letting your fear take over, you hopped on, and before you knew it, that fear was completely gone as you were having fun!

Our emotions come and go. When we realize how much God loves us, we feel love, joy, and thankfulness. But on days when we don't have those feelings, we should stay faithful to Him. Why? Because we are committed—we have given our lives to Jesus. On days when we can't seem to feel God's love for us or our love for Him, we choose to live God's way regardless. Even though we might be laughed at, we still walk away from friends using bad language. Even though we may not feel like it, we still stand up for someone other kids are teasing.

While feelings come and go, commitment stays. And it overcomes negative emotions like doubt and fear. Keep on showing God you love Him, no matter what you're feeling. He's committed to loving you! His "faithfulness reaches to the clouds" (Psalm 36:5)!

A HIGHER DESTINY

The way of the L<small>ORD</small> is strength for the upright.

PROVERBS 10:29

Parents provide for their children and are happy to spend time with them. They love their kids, and they want their kids to love them back and be loyal.

God is our heavenly Father, and He wants us to be His loyal and loving children. And because we are His children, He is also happy to spend time with us.

The story of the prodigal son (you can read it in Luke 15:11–32) tells us how much God wants to have a strong and loving relationship with us. If His children wander far from Him, He longs for them to come home and be near to Him again. God knows that His ways are best and give us strength.

All through the Bible God is constantly saying, "Return to Me, and I will return to you." No matter how far we have strayed, God still loves us, and He wants to welcome us home—forever.

THE BIBLE IS TRUE

Your word, O Lord, is eternal; it stands firm in the heavens.
PSALM 119:89 NIV

If your friends are talking about a book you haven't read yet, you might say to them, "Don't tell me how it ends! I want to be surprised." Knowing how the story ends would spoil your enjoyment of the book.

But with the Bible, knowing how the story ends makes the book even better! So when we hear news reports about frightening things happening in the world, we don't need to worry. These things are the consequences of sin. The prophet Jeremiah said, "The heart is deceitful above all things, and desperately wicked" (Jeremiah 17:9). But God has a plan to deal with sin, and He is in control.

Never forget: God will speak history's final word. Every day the world moves closer to the time when Christ will return, Satan will be defeated, and God's perfect plan will be fulfilled.

No matter how frightening the future may look at times, God's Word, the Bible, tells us how the story will end—and it will be wonderful! Don't lose heart. The best is yet to be!

VALUABLE TO GOD

He who trusts in his riches will fall, but the
righteous will flourish like foliage.
PROVERBS 11:28

A successful, rich man died, and at his funeral, curious friends asked
one another, "How much money did he leave?"

"He left it all," someone replied, and everyone was very impressed.
What an important and amazing man!

But God doesn't judge us like that—by our success or how much
money we have. He loves each person the same. Your value to God
doesn't come from what you do, the clothes you wear, or the house you
live in. Your value comes from the facts that God made you and loves
you and that Jesus died for you. When we receive Jesus and God adopts
us into His family, we become His children forever.

Possessions and popularity don't define who you are, and you can't
take those to Heaven with you. Understand your value to God and get
your identity from Jesus. You are more important to Him than you'll
ever know!

VICTORY IN JESUS

Thanks be to God, who gives us the victory through our Lord Jesus Christ.
1 CORINTHIANS 15:57 NRSV

Joseph Haydn, a great classical composer, was once asked why his church music was so cheerful. He replied, "When I think upon God, my heart is so full of joy that the notes dance and leap, as it were, from my pen, and since God has given me a cheerful heart . . . I serve Him with a cheerful spirit."

Haydn had discovered the secret to lasting joy: "I think on God." Putting all our focus on our current situation in life won't bring us lasting joy. It might even make us feel angry or sad. But when we "think on God"—when we turn our minds and hearts to God's power and His love for us, we can't help but be joyful. The apostle Paul said, "Set your mind on things above, not on things on the earth" (Colossians 3:2).

Every day brings temptations, but Jesus gives us the strength we need to have victory over them. We can be like the girl who said that when the Devil came knocking with a temptation, she just sent Jesus to answer the door!

LOOK TO GOD

"Lift up your heads, because your redemption draws near."

LUKE 21:28

I f you've ever flown in an airplane, you know that you see planet Earth much differently from high in the air than you do on the ground. Your view, or *perspective*, changes. Pictures taken from the moon and from space have an even different perspective.

God wants to give us a change of perspective too. As we look to God, instead of to ourselves and our problems, our perspective changes.

When a friend is mad at you or you need to forgive someone who made you mad, you see only your own problems, but God sees the whole picture. He sees the present and the future too. He wants us to see our problems with His perspective. Israel's King David said, "The LORD will perfect that which concerns me" (Psalm 138:8).

So look up! Don't get bogged down. Keep your eyes on God—He sees the whole picture, and He knows what is best for you. You can trust Him, because He loves you.

A SOLID FOUNDATION

The LORD is my rock and my fortress and my deliverer.
2 SAMUEL 22:2

My children used to sing a song in Sunday school that began, "The wise man built his house upon the rock . . ." You might have sung this song too. Wise people do build their lives upon the Rock—the Lord Jesus and His Word. No other foundation will last.

In big cities I often see wrecking balls destroying old structures to make way for new ones. Some of these "old structures" in America are less than a hundred years old. In Europe and other parts of the world, buildings several centuries old—and even older—are common. But even those buildings will eventually fall apart.

Jesus said, "Everyone who hears these words of mine and puts them into practice is like a wise man who built his house on the rock" (Matthew 7:24 NIV). Only a life built on the solid foundation of God's Word will last.

Are you listening to God's Word and putting it into practice every day?

GENTLE KINDNESS

A servant of the Lord must not quarrel but be gentle to all.
2 TIMOTHY 2:24

Wherever true Christians have gone, they have shown kindness, love, and gentleness. Around the world, Christians have built hospitals, orphanages, schools, and shelters for homeless people. They have provided supplies to help people recover from floods and earthquakes. Jesus' followers look for ways to show kindness to everyone, no matter who they are or where they live.

Jesus healed the sick, fed the hungry, and opened the eyes of the blind. He taught His disciples, "Love your neighbor as yourself" (Matthew 19:19), and told them to follow what we have come to call the Golden Rule: "In everything, do to others what you would have them do to you" (Matthew 7:12 NIV).

Jesus was strong, but He was also kind and gentle. Do others see His gentleness and compassion in you?

JULY 25

NO COMPLAINING

"In the world you will have tribulation; but be of
good cheer, I have overcome the world."
JOHN 16:33

When troubles come, we sometimes act as if God is on vacation. We ask, "Why is this happening to me? What did I do to deserve this?"

Read the promises of the Bible for the answer. Jesus said, "In the world you will have tribulation." *Tribulation* means "trouble." Jesus didn't say that tribulation comes to bad people only—He said *everyone* will experience trouble.

So such complaining is shortsighted and wrong. God is far higher than we are. Who are we to say He is wrong or to tell Him what He ought to be doing? As God reminded Job, "Where were you when I laid the foundations of the earth?" (Job 38:4). When we complain, we are doubting God's wisdom and His love for us.

Instead of complaining, read the promises of Scripture for the answer: "Be of good cheer, I have overcome the world." Jesus will help you.

JOY EVERY DAY

The joy of the Lord is your strength.
NEHEMIAH 8:10

Young or old, all Christians can serve Jesus with their talents, skills, and spiritual gifts. But sometimes we get discouraged when we see other believers getting special attention for their service while we are not. When this happens, we miss the service opportunities that God is giving *us*. We forget that we are here to serve Jesus, not ourselves.

You don't need to try to be like the popular cheerleader or football player or anyone else who gets a lot of attention. You just need to be yourself—your best self, with Jesus' help. Develop the abilities and interests that He gives to you. God made you for a purpose. The key is to realize you are here to serve Him, not yourself.

God never promises that life will be perfect. But every day, as we serve Jesus, we truly discover that the joy of the Lord is our strength.

A VICTORIOUS CHRISTIAN

The Spirit also helps in our weaknesses.
ROMANS 8:26

Did you know that the Holy Spirit prays for you? Romans 8:26 says, "The Spirit helps us. We are very weak, but the Spirit helps us with our weakness. We do not know how to pray as we should. But the Spirit himself speaks to God for us, even begs God for us. The Spirit speaks to God with deep feelings that words cannot explain" (ICB).

We need to rely constantly on the Holy Spirit. We need to remember that Jesus lives inside us through the Holy Spirit! We have to choose between good and bad every day. Why *don't* we rely on God the way we should?

Sometimes we don't realize how weak we are and how easy it is for us to make the wrong choice. We forget how strong our enemy is. We might even doubt if God is really going to help us. Or we think we can fix everything ourselves. But we should ask the Holy Spirit to do it all and to take over in all our choices and decisions.

What are you worried about today? Remember that God is in control and will be victorious in the end. Whatever your difficulties, whatever your circumstances, remember that Jesus is ready to help you!

FREE TO CHOOSE

Choose this day whom you will serve.

JOSHUA 24:15 NRSV

Y ou make decisions every day. Sometimes they are easy and not very important—will you wear the red shirt or the blue one today? But sometimes your decisions are tougher. Will you quit the team because you're not a starter? Will you help your friend cheat on the big test?

When we face decisions, we need to remember that God hasn't left us in the dark and that He is very interested in our situations and choices. God loves us, and He wants what is best for us. He has a perfect path in life for us, and He wants us to choose His way instead of the wrong way Satan tempts us to go.

God gives us light to help us see the right way. He gives us His Word, the Bible—and many of our decisions become easier when we follow God's Word. God also gives us wisdom, sometimes through other people, to understand our situation, and He gives us the Holy Spirit to guide us.

God gives you freedom to choose. Never make a decision without giving it to God and seeking His will. He promises to guide you—and He will.

SIMPLE TRUST

Trust in the LORD with all your heart, and lean
not on your own understanding.
PROVERBS 3:5

God knows everything; we do not. Only in Heaven will we understand God's ways better than we do now.

But the Bible tells us a lot about God's character—what He is like and what He does. We know that God loves us. We know we can trust that God always does what is best for us. God says in His Word, "I know the plans I have for you . . . plans to prosper you and not to harm you, plans to give you hope and a future" (Jeremiah 29:11 NIV).

Corrie ten Boom once compared this to the experience of looking at a piece of embroidery—a piece of art made with thread and cloth. On the back, you see mostly knots and loose threads. On the front, you see a beautiful design. Right now we can only see the back, while God sees the front!

God is in control. Whatever happens today, you can confidently say, "[I] know that all things work together for good to those who love God, to those who are the called according to His purpose" (Romans 8:28).

THE LIGHT OF LIFE

Your faith and hope are in God.

1 PETER 1:21 NIV

Have you ever lost something very important to you? Maybe it was a special gift or a trophy.

Sometimes Christians lose something very important—we lose sight of Heaven. We can get so used to our everyday lives in this world that we don't think about what's coming next. We get used to hearing about trouble in the world and forget that Jesus said, "I am the light of the world. He who follows Me shall not walk in darkness, but have the light of life" (John 8:12).

Jesus' light makes Him the Hope of the hopeless, the Savior of the lost, and the Guide of the wandering. Jesus alone is "the Lamb of God who takes away the sin of the world!" (John 1:29). He alone "reflects the glory of God," shows us what God is like, and "holds everything together with his powerful word" (Hebrews 1:3 ICB).

All over the world, leaders, families, and even children like you struggle with problems—and you always will. But when things look dark, remember Jesus' light. He alone is the Hope of the world—and He is your Hope as well.

EFFECTIVE PRAYER

"Before they call, I will answer; and while they
are still speaking, I will hear."
ISAIAH 65:24

John Knox spent much time in prayer, and the church in Scotland burst into new life. John Wesley prayed long and often, and the Methodist church movement was born. Martin Luther prayed earnestly, and the Reformation (the movement that formed the Protestant church) exploded across Europe. Why was prayer so important to these men of the past?

Knox, Wesley, and Luther knew they were up against strong forces of spiritual opposition. They also knew how important it is for people to hear the gospel message. Like the apostle Paul, they could say, "We use God's mighty weapons, not worldly weapons, to knock down the strongholds of human reasoning and to destroy false arguments" (2 Corinthians 10:4 NLT).

Our world is the same today. God still wants Christians to be concerned about lost people. Prayer is one of His weapons for sharing the gospel all over the earth. "The earnest prayer of a righteous person has great power and produces wonderful results" (James 5:16 NLT). Will you pray for someone to hear the gospel today?

AUGUST

Don't worry about anything; instead, pray about everything.
PHILIPPIANS 4:6 TLB

PRAYER RELEASES GOD'S POWER

Pray all the time.
1 THESSALONIANS 5:17 THE MESSAGE

Sometimes people say, "All I can do is pray." They make it sound like their prayers won't have any effect. All I can do is pray?! You might as well say to a starving man, "All I can do is give you food."

Prayer isn't something to use only in an emergency. Prayer releases the power of God. James 4:2 says, "You do not have because you do not ask." The apostle Paul wrote, "Do not be anxious about anything, but in everything, by prayer and petition, with thanksgiving, present your requests to God" (Philippians 4:6 NIV).

This is true not only for our own needs but for the needs of others too. So often our prayers focus only on ourselves. But God wants to use us, through our prayers, to change the lives of other people as well.

Who should you be praying for today?

CHOOSE LIFE

I have set before you life and death, . . . therefore choose life.
DEUTERONOMY 30:19

In the early years of the space program, helicopters picked up astronauts whose space capsules had parachuted into the sea as they returned from space. A tiny spacecraft would be located in the enormous ocean, and the astronauts would be lifted out of their capsule into the helicopter, which then flew them to the safety of a nearby ship.

As I've watched those scenes on television, they've made me think of how God is with us. God hovers over the entire world, always seeking to pull people out of sin. He tosses out a line to all who are in danger of "drowning."

Some grab on to God's rescue line and freely receive the gift of His Son, Jesus. They have been pulled to safety, so to speak, and at the end of their earthly lives, they will go to Heaven. But others ignore the line or even knock it away. They don't believe they are really in danger, or they think they can make it to safety on their own. Tragically, they are lost, not because God rejected them, but because they rejected God.

Accepting God's rescue plan or rejecting it—which choice do you think is the better one?

CHRIST, OUR EXAMPLE

He learned obedience by the things which He suffered.
HEBREWS 5:8

The main reason Jesus died on the cross was to save us from our sins. But the New Testament also teaches that His suffering was important as an example for us.

The Greek word for *example* comes from school life in ancient times. It refers to something written down by the teacher so it could be copied exactly by a child learning to write. Jesus is our copybook. We look to Him as our teacher, and we follow His example. We can learn how to handle suffering by looking at what He did.

All people everywhere will suffer at some point in their lives. How did Jesus bear it? By not giving in to hopelessness or doubt. By looking beyond it and seeing the joy that was to come. By knowing the Father was with Him and would use the suffering for good.

When we face suffering, we can remember and follow Jesus' example. "Consider him who endured such opposition from sinful men, so that you will not grow weary and lose heart" (Hebrews 12:3 NIV).

PATIENCE AND PERFECTION

The testing of your faith produces patience.
JAMES 1:3

When is it hardest for you to be patient? Waiting for your birthday or Christmas? Waiting while your mom shops? Waiting to find out your grade on a test? Patience isn't easy for most of us.

The Bible tells us, "Be patient . . . until the Lord's coming. See how the farmer waits for the land to yield its valuable crop and how patient he is for the autumn and spring rains. You too, be patient and stand firm, because the Lord's coming is near" (James 5:7–8 NIV). When our faith is being tested, this is very good advice!

Patience is an attitude of expecting something good to happen. The farmer patiently works and watches his land because he expects crops to grow. When something or someone tests our faith, we can expect something good to come from it. We can see the situation as an opportunity to trust God more patiently.

Ask God for the gift of patience—and then use it!

AUGUST 5

PEACE ON EARTH?

He Himself is our peace.
EPHESIANS 2:14

In 1956, Jim Elliott and four other missionaries lost their lives to the fierce Auca people of Ecuador. The missionaries had befriended these warriors, hoping to present the gospel to them, because the missionaries knew the only way to stop the killing was for the Aucas to come to Jesus. And despite the missionaries' deaths, that did happen!

Less than two years after Jim Elliott's death, his wife and daughter and the sister of one of the other missionaries went to live with the Aucas. Many Aucas became Christians, and they are now a peaceful, friendly tribe.

Conflict still exists on earth among nations, communities, and families. Special prizes and organizations have been created, much money and time have been spent, treaties have been signed, books have been written . . . but no human formula has been found to bring peace on earth.

What can be done? The only solution is the one God offers—His Son, Jesus. He is the only One who can end conflict by changing our hearts and giving us His peace and love for others.

The next time you are in the middle of a conflict, remember Jesus is our Peace, and ask Him for His help.

A HAPPY HOME

Children are a gift from the LORD; they are a reward from him.

PSALM 127:3 NLT

No achievement in life is greater than building a happy home and raising successful children who love Jesus. Parents' main job is to be sure their children grow up in a home where God is honored and Jesus' love is shared.

It's a lot of work to take care of children and help them grow. Think about all the different ways your parents provide for you, take care of you, and help you every day. And on top of all that, they also teach you—how to do chores, what's right and wrong, how to have good manners. Your mom or dad might coach your team and help you get better at your sport. They might teach you a special skill or hobby, like woodworking or quilting. But the most important thing Christian parents teach their children is how much God loves us and how He wants us to live to show that we love Him back.

The Bible says children are a gift from the Lord. If you are tempted to disobey your parents, stop and think—what kind of gift do you want to be?

PRAY ABOUT YOUR PROBLEMS

Don't worry about anything; instead, pray about everything.
PHILIPPIANS 4:6 TLB

What do you do when you have a problem? Do you worry? Most of us do. But does worrying ever solve the problem? No. So if worry doesn't solve the problem, why worry? Maybe there's a better way!

In the Bible, a king named Hezekiah gives us an idea for problem solving. An enemy of his kingdom sent Hezekiah a threatening letter. After Hezekiah read it, he "went up to the house of the LORD, and spread it before the LORD. Then Hezekiah prayed before the LORD" (2 Kings 19:14–15).

Hezekiah was calm. He didn't freeze. He didn't worry. Instead, he turned to God right away. Sometimes we pray to God as a last resort. Hezekiah prayed first. His example is better!

When you have a problem, turn to God right away. He cares for you, and He will show you what to do.

THE PROBLEM OF SUFFERING

I have kept His way and not turned aside.
JOB 23:11

When you need an answer to a question for a school report, you look in your textbook or search at the library or online. Some questions about life, however, just don't have answers, at least not here on earth. One of those questions is: Why does God allow suffering?

The book of Job, which may be the oldest book in the Bible, deals with this hard question. How can God be loving and good *and* let people suffer? To put it another way, we may think, *If God lets us suffer, He must not love us.* But that is not true. God *does* love us—and the proof is the suffering He allowed His Son to face on the cross.

So what is the answer to this age-old question? The key is to understand the character of God. That is what Job discovered when he was suffering and wanted to know why. God didn't give Job a complete answer, but He helped Job realize that He could be trusted, because He is merciful and loving.

You can trust God too—not because He always gives us all the answers, but simply because He is God.

AUGUST 9

JESUS' PRAYER PROGRAM

"Whatever you ask the Father in My name He will give you."
JOHN 16:23

Do you have someone you love to talk to? Maybe it's your best friend, or your mom or dad, or a favorite cousin or grandparent. When you are together, you never run out of things to talk about. Did you know that praying can be like that?

One of the most amazing things about Jesus' life is how much time He spent in prayer. He had only three years of ministry, yet He was never too hurried to spend hours in prayer. Jesus praised and thanked God often. He prayed before every difficult task. He prayed every day, and sometimes He prayed all night. No one could have been busier—but He was never too busy for prayer.

Too often our prayers are quick and careless. We might repeat a few memorized verses in the morning before we hurry out the door. Then we'll say good-bye to God for the rest of the day until we rush through a few requests at night. This isn't how Jesus prayed.

Stop and think: What keeps you from praying more every day?

TRUST AND OBEY

As the body without the spirit is dead, so faith without works is dead also.

JAMES 2:26

On a sports team, everyone's position is important. Everyone has a part in achieving the goal of winning the game.

In God's kingdom, everyone has a part too. Our part is to believe God and to follow Him. We trust Jesus as our Savior and obey Him as our Lord. That is a summary of *discipleship*—believing and following.

The New Testament makes no separation between belief and obedience. The two are linked together. If we truly believe, we will follow. Trusting Jesus makes us part of God's kingdom. Our love for God and our obedience to His will show that we are citizens of that kingdom. We show our faith by what we do.

That is why being a Christian is a happy blend of trusting and working, resting and trying, receiving and doing. God does His part, and we do ours. A farmer's crop is a gift from God—but it also requires hard work. God might give a person the gift of music—but it takes practice and discipline to make it come alive.

Can others see your faith by what you do? Believe—and obey.

AUGUST 11

GOD, OUR FATHER

"I will be a Father to you, and you shall be My sons and daughters."
2 CORINTHIANS 6:18

Have you ever had to pick a prize? There were several to choose from, but you couldn't tell from the wrappings what they were. Did you wonder if one of the prizes would be better and more exciting than the rest and try to choose that one?

In Jesus' story of the prodigal son, the younger son wasn't satisfied in his father's house with all his needs met. He wanted more. He believed the lie that something more exciting was waiting for him away from his father.

Isn't this how we sometimes behave? We think God is holding out on us, that there is something better than a close relationship with our heavenly Father, that the world offers more excitement and joy than He does. But it isn't true. As the prodigal son found out, when we think this way and then act on it, we always end up wishing we hadn't. We always end up needing to ask for God's help and forgiveness.

Our heavenly Father always answers us with love and mercy. But wouldn't it have been far better to have avoided the trouble in the first place? Don't ever think Satan's way is better than God's way—it never is.

THE HOPE OF HEAVEN

Precious in the sight of the LORD is the death of His saints.

PSALM 116:15

Sometimes when Christians are at the end of their lives, God gives them a special glimpse of Heaven. I believe one reason He does this is to encourage those of us who remain on earth. Just before dying, my grandmother sat up in bed, smiled, and said, "I see Jesus, and He has His hand outstretched to me. And there is Ben, and he has both of his eyes and both of his legs." (Ben, my grandfather, had lost an eye and a leg at the Battle of Gettysburg during the Civil War.)

Most young people don't think much about dying. You are too busy living every day and preparing for your future. That is how it should be. But death *is* part of life on earth. Your first experience with death might be the death of a neighbor or a family member.

For believers death isn't something to be feared. We know it is the entrance to our life with God in Heaven. No wonder the apostle Paul declared, "I desire to depart and be with Christ, which is better by far" (Philippians 1:23 NIV).

EVERLASTING LOVE

"I have loved you with an everlasting love; therefore
with lovingkindness I have drawn you."
JEREMIAH 31:3

John 3:16 might be the best known verse of the Bible: "For God so loved the world that He gave His only begotten Son, that whoever believes in Him should not perish but have eternal life." Who can describe or measure the love of God? God *is* love. Throughout the Bible we learn of God's love. Through Jesus' death and resurrection, His presence with us, His future return——these tell us of the power and the promise of God's love.

God shows His love to us every day, with great kindness. He gives the sunshine and rain we need for our food to grow. He paints beautiful sunrises and sunsets in the sky. He gives us family and friends to care for us. He gives us smiles and laughter when we see puppies and kittens. He gives us music that makes us feel joy.

No matter what our sins, no matter how terrible they may be, God loves us. He loves us with an everlasting love. The proof? Jesus Christ, God's only Son, went to the cross for us.

ANGELS PRAISE GOD

Bless the LORD, you His angels, who excel in strength, who do His word.

PSALM 103:20

A t a football game, when a new president is elected, when the Oscars are given out, people cheer to show their approval and support. But no one deserves our praise more than God!

The Bible says the angels do much more than help *us*. They offer continual praise to God, giving glory to His name and rejoicing in His holiness and perfection.

The prophet Isaiah saw a vision of Heaven, where angelic hosts proclaim, "Holy, holy, holy is the LORD of hosts; the whole earth is full of His glory!" (Isaiah 6:3). The apostle John saw "many angels around the throne . . . saying with a loud voice: 'Worthy is the Lamb who was slain'" (Revelation 5:11–12). Jesus said there is "rejoicing in the presence of the angels of God over one sinner who repents" (Luke 15:10 NIV). These are examples for us to follow.

Are rejoicing and praise natural and important parts of your life? Praise chases away worry and fear and brings us closer to God. How could you praise Him right now?

AUGUST 15

FULL SURRENDER

"Whoever loses his life for My sake . . . will save it."
MARK 8:35

A police sergeant once asked me the secret of victorious Christian living. I told him there is no magic formula, but if any one word could describe it, it would be *surrender*. To surrender means to give in or give up, to let someone else have power and control. When we come to Jesus, we surrender our lives to Him.

You might ask, "How can I surrender my life?" The answer is that we give God control. Rather than choosing to do what we want, we listen to God and His Word and choose to do what He wants. We confess our sin and give every situation in our lives to Jesus.

It's not enough to tell Jesus one time that you love Him. We can't live the rest of our lives in the glow of that experience. We need to have regular spiritual checkups. Are we getting to know God better? Are we trusting Him more? Are we doing what He says to do? Are we loving and serving others?

Jesus said, "If anyone desires to come after Me, let him deny himself, and take up his cross daily, and follow Me" (Luke 9:23). Daily surrender—that's the key to daily victory.

HEARTFELT PRAYER

"If My people . . . will . . . pray and seek My
face, . . . I will hear from heaven."
2 CHRONICLES 7:14

From one end of the Bible to the other, we can read the stories of people whose prayers God heard and answered. The prayers of these men and women changed history.

The prophet Elijah prayed in front of God's enemies, and God sent fire from Heaven to show that He is truly God. Elisha prayed, and a woman's young son was raised from the dead. Hannah prayed, and God gave her a baby, who grew to be the prophet Samuel and led God's people for many years.

Paul prayed, and dozens of new churches grew strong. Peter prayed, and a woman named Dorcas was raised to life, ready to serve Jesus again.

All these prayers and more came from the faith of the people who prayed. They wanted their lives to count for God's glory, and they prayed big prayers that only He could answer. Is there a big, heartfelt prayer that you can pray today?

LORD AND MASTER

"You call Me Teacher and Lord, and you say well, for so I am."
JOHN 13:13

I wonder if you've ever thought about the incredible number of messages that surround you every day. They come to you in TV and website ads, magazines, song lyrics, what people say in movies, and what your friends tell you. The list is almost endless.

How many of the messages you receive each day shape your thinking? How many of them start to convince you that the way to be happy is to have the latest and greatest game? How many of them persuade you that the most important thing in life is what others think of you or what you own?

It's hard to resist the impact of so many messages! But God says our thinking must be shaped by His truth. What this world calls valuable, God calls worthless. What this world looks down on, God praises. "My thoughts are not your thoughts, nor are your ways My ways" (Isaiah 55:8).

Jesus said, "You call Me Teacher and Lord, and you say well, for so I am." Is He your Teacher and Lord—or do you listen to the wrong messages?

HOPE FOR THE HEART

My heart is glad, and . . . my flesh also will rest in hope.

PSALM 16:9

A famous heart surgeon, Dr. McNair Wilson, once said, "Hope is the medicine I use more than any other—hope can cure nearly anything." Perhaps the greatest need all people have is the need for hope. The Bible tells us the importance of hope, and even scientific experiments have proven that hope is good medicine.

In the midst of our problems, we can *wish* for a better life, but *hope* means believing that something better is coming. In the Bible, hope means being certain that God does all things well. It means knowing that what God tells us in the Bible is true, and that God keeps all His promises.

When we come to Jesus, we have hope—hope for eternity, and hope for a better life today, right now, because He is with us.

Do you have hope today? True hope comes only from Jesus.

LOVED|

In this is love, not that we loved God, but that He loved us.
1 JOHN 4:10

Mister Rogers often spoke about the power of love. He said that "knowing that we can be loved exactly as we are gives us all the best opportunity for growing into the healthiest of people."

But sadly, many people go through life feeling unloved—and unlovable. Perhaps they were constantly criticized or ignored as children, or their families faced conflict. Perhaps as teenagers they made bad choices about important issues, and now they feel unworthy of love. Maybe you know someone who feels like this, or maybe you do yourself.

But listen: I have good news! No matter the reason, your feelings aren't telling you the truth! God loves you! Begin to see yourself the way God sees you, and your attitudes about yourself will begin to change. If Jesus didn't love you, would He have been willing to die for you? The Bible says, "By this we know love, because He laid down His life for us" (1 John 3:16).

God loves you. Hammer that truth into your heart and mind every day. It will make all the difference!

FACING REJECTION

He is despised and rejected by men, a Man of
sorrows and acquainted with grief.
ISAIAH 53:3

Have you ever been criticized or rejected? Maybe you struck out or missed a goal and your teammates were angry. Maybe your entry in the art contest made everyone laugh.

Throughout His earthly life, Jesus often had to deal with people criticizing and rejecting Him. The people in His hometown tried to throw Him off a cliff (Luke 4:29). The religious and political leaders argued with Him, wanted to kill Him, and brought Him to trial before Pilate and Herod, and then He was crucified.

Sometimes when people point out how we are wrong or weak, it can help us learn to be better people. But Jesus had done nothing wrong, and He wasn't weak! How did He respond?

First, He never stopped doing what He knew was right. Second, He stayed strong and courageous. He was headed toward the cross, which He knew was God's will. Third, He didn't argue or fight. King Herod prodded Jesus to defend Himself, but He chose not to say anything. Jesus cared about only one thing: doing what God wanted Him to do.

No matter what people around you say, follow Jesus' example and keep doing what God wants you to do.

MEEK?

"Blessed are the meek, for they shall inherit the earth."
MATTHEW 5:5

People don't use the word *meek* much today, but Jesus said meekness is important in God's kingdom. What does it mean to be meek?

First, meekness is *not* weakness, or being easily frightened, or letting people push you around. Meekness is trusting God to work and having a loving, patient, and gentle attitude toward others.

Moses became meek as God worked in his life over a forty-year period in the wilderness.

There was a time when the apostle Peter said and did the first thing that came into his mind. But little by little, after Jesus' resurrection, the Holy Spirit transformed Peter and made him meek.

Before Paul became a Christian, he wasn't meek. His job was to persecute Christians! Yet later he wrote, "The fruit of the Spirit is . . . gentleness, goodness, . . . meekness" (Galatians 5:22–23 KJV).

No one is naturally meek. We all want our own way. Only the Holy Spirit can change our lives, making us more like Jesus—our example of true meekness.

HEAVEN IS REAL

God will wipe away every tear from their eyes.
REVELATION 7:17

In Iowa an artist named Pat Acton makes amazing models of places using only matchsticks—usually several hundred thousand! His detailed models of the new World Trade Center and the International Space Station accurately show what these places look like. The artist calls his models "Matchstick Marvels."

We don't know what Heaven looks like, but we know it is a marvelous place. In addition to being beautiful beyond what we can imagine now, Heaven is the place where all the problems of earth will be forgotten. God promises that in Heaven "there shall be no more death, nor sorrow, nor crying. There shall be no more pain, for the former things have passed away" (Revelation 21:4).

Heaven is real, and God's promises are true. Jesus and His church—everyone who is part of God's kingdom—will live together there forever. We can look forward to the future because we know Heaven is ahead of us!

TRULY TRANSFORMED

Present your bodies a living sacrifice. . . . And
do not be conformed to this world.
ROMANS 12:1–2

Sports umpires and referees use arm movements to signal their calls during a game. The red, green, and yellow lights on a traffic signal tell drivers to stop, go forward, or prepare to stop. Signals are all around us.

Our actions act as signals too. They tell others about what is going on inside us. A frown signals worry, a smile signals happiness, and a thumbs-up signals that something is good. Our actions also tell others about our commitment to Jesus. This is why the Bible tells us to give our bodies to God as an offering of worship. Whatever it is our bodies are doing, we want them to be honoring God.

People will judge what you are on the inside by what they see happening on the outside. We may claim to follow Jesus, but if our actions tell a different story, people have a right to question our claim. How we dress, how we talk, and how we act daily all should honor God. We are to be "blameless and pure, children of God without fault" (Philippians 2:15 NIV).

How about you? Do your outer actions signal that you are living for Jesus?

PURE IN HEART

"Blessed are the pure in heart, for they shall see God."

MATTHEW 5:8

What did Jesus mean when He said we should be "pure in heart"? A pure heart wants what God wants. The reason is because our heart—our inner being—is the root of all our actions. From our hearts come our motives, our desires, our goals, our emotions.

All our actions come from our hearts—our inner selves. If our hearts aren't right, our actions won't be either. Jesus put it this way: "All these evil things begin inside a person . . . stealing, murder, . . . selfishness, doing bad things to other people, lying, . . . jealousy, saying bad things about people, pride, and foolish living" (Mark 7:21–22 ICB). Not a very pretty picture!

But when we come to God in faith and ask for forgiveness, He makes us pure through Jesus. "The blood of Jesus Christ His Son cleanses us from all sin" (1 John 1:7). Then day by day, as we follow the Holy Spirit, He helps us turn from evil and seek what is good.

God wants to give you a pure heart—and He will. "Blessed are the pure in heart."

GOD HOLDS US

The eternal God is your refuge.
DEUTERONOMY 33:27

Have you ever noticed that people are almost always smiling in TV commercials? The advertisers want you to believe that if you use their product, you will always be happy. In fact, watching only commercials could make you think that people are always happy and smiling! But that's just not true.

When we hear the word *suffering* we usually think of physical pain. But our emotions, like sadness or fear, can cause real suffering too.

The apostle Paul experienced this kind of suffering. He wrote to the church in Corinth "out of great distress and anguish of heart" (2 Corinthians 2:4 NIV). Jesus, in the Garden of Gethsemane before the crucifixion, "being in agony, . . . prayed more earnestly" (Luke 22:44). After denying his Lord three times, Peter "went out and wept bitterly" (Luke 22:62).

These kinds of times come to everyone. When they do, God still loves us! And He wants to help us. "The eternal God is your refuge, and underneath are the everlasting arms" (Deuteronomy 33:27).

GOD IS OUR STRENGTH

The Lord is my light and my salvation; whom shall I fear?

PSALM 27:1

D o you sometimes feel afraid? What frightens you? What do you do when you are afraid?

It is a fact that God is our light and our salvation. That means He shows us what to do, and He saves us. God is a "very present help in trouble" (Psalm 46:1), and He fears nothing!

We can trust that the all-powerful, all-knowing, all-loving God of the universe is able to deliver us from all sorts of trouble. He wants to give us strength to overcome temptations to sin. He wants to give us courage to face our problems instead of avoiding them. He wants to help us find the practical wisdom and help we need to deal with problems and fears. Everyone feels fear at times. But God says we don't need to give in to our fears; He will give us strength.

What do you fear today? Whatever it is, ask God to help you turn your fear over to Him. "The Lord is my light and my salvation—so why should I be afraid?" (Psalm 27:1 NLT).

NEVER THE SAME AGAIN

"I will give them a new heart and a new mind."
EZEKIEL 11:19 GNT

Everyone loves a good story, and some of the best ones are about people whose lives changed in big ways when Jesus became their Savior.

Some of us are born to Christian parents who teach us about God from the time we're very young. Others don't grow up knowing Jesus. But every day, all over the world, people meet Jesus. And when they do, they can never be the same again.

When Jesus was crucified, two other men were crucified at the same time. Both were thieves. One of these dying men was drawn to the warmth of the Savior; he responded to Jesus in faith and was saved. The other dying man rejected Jesus; he was lost forever.

God makes weak people strong. He makes evil people clean. He takes the sinful and makes them pure.

With this in mind, Ezekiel said, "The Lord spoke to me. . . . 'I will give them a new heart and a new mind. I will take away their stubborn heart of stone and will give them an obedient heart'" (Ezekiel 11:14, 19 GNT).

You will never be the same once you know Jesus. What difference will He make in your life today?

AN ATTITUDE OF GRATITUDE

Let the peace of Christ rule in your hearts. . . . And be thankful.

COLOSSIANS 3:15 NIV

Long ago a minister named Matthew Henry was robbed. He wrote in his diary, "Let me be thankful first because I was never robbed before; second, although they took my [bag], they did not take my life; third, because although they took my all, it was not much; and fourth, because it was I who was robbed, not I who robbed." I wonder if I could be that thankful if I were robbed!

Thankfulness isn't our usual response when something goes wrong. We may have a hundred good things to be thankful for—but let one bad thing happen, and it's all we think about!

The Bible says, "In everything give thanks" (1 Thessalonians 5:18). No matter what happens, we are to give thanks. So develop a habit of thanking God each day. Thank God for every blessing He gives you. Thank Him for Jesus and what He has done for you. Even when things go wrong, thank Him that He is still good and you are still in His care.

Do you have an attitude of thankfulness every day?

AUGUST 29

PERFECT PEACE

The love of God has been poured out in our hearts
by the Holy Spirit who was given to us.
ROMANS 5:5

Years ago when I traveled to Europe to preach, I liked to travel by sea and enjoy five days of quiet on the ship.

On one of my voyages, a captain took me down to see the ship's gyroscope. "When the sea is rough," he said, "the gyroscope helps to keep the ship on an even keel (well-balanced and steady). Though the waves may reach tremendous proportions, the gyroscope helps to stabilize the vessel."

As I listened, I thought about how the Holy Spirit is like a gyroscope. No matter what happens, our souls will be kept on an even keel, in perfect peace, when the Holy Spirit lives in our hearts.

Problems and disappointments, temptations and testing will come like a storm. Our enemy, Satan, will come at us like a flood. But the Spirit comforts us with His presence and assures us that God's love and His promises are true.

DIAMONDS IN THE DARK

Blessed is the man who fears the Lord, who
delights greatly in His commandments.
PSALM 112:1

Have you ever seen a diamond ring? Did it shine? Jewelers often place diamonds on dark velvet cloths when they show the diamonds to customers. The dark background shows off the cut and sparkle of the stone.

Christians should stand out like sparkling diamonds against a dark background. We should be wholesome, courteous, full of laughter and joy, but firm in the things we do or do not do. Jesus meant for His followers to be different from the world—and if we are truly following Him, we will be.

But just being different is not enough. There's a purpose for who we are and how we live. We are to be the kindest, the most unselfish, the friendliest, the hardest working, the most thoughtful, the truest, and the most loving people on earth.

The Bible says, "Those who are wise will shine like the brightness of the heavens, and those who lead many to righteousness, like the stars for ever and ever" (Daniel 12:3 NIV). Ask God to help you be different from the world so you shine like a star for Jesus.

NEVER BE BORED

There remains therefore a rest for the people of God.
HEBREWS 4:9

When you have free time with no responsibilities, when your chores and homework are done, what do you usually do? Ride your bike? Play a game? Listen to music or watch a movie?

This is the most entertained generation in history. Large screen TVs pull in hundreds of channels. Professional sports teams take in (and spend) billions of dollars. Children are upset if they don't get the latest video games for Christmas. Our smartphones are always on.

I believe this frantic search for entertainment is a symptom of something deeper. Some have suggested we are the most bored generation in history—and perhaps that is right. Down inside is an empty place in our hearts—a restlessness, a search for inner peace—that just won't go away. And the more we try to satisfy it with entertainment, the less content we become.

Only Jesus can fill that empty space in our hearts, and He will. As we open our lives to Him and serve Him and other people, we aren't bored or empty. But God's Word also points us to the future—to Heaven, where our hearts will have complete peace. "There remains therefore a rest for the people of God."

SEPTEMBER

The LORD is good; His mercy is everlasting.

PSALM 100:5

SEPTEMBER 1

A TIME APART

The eyes of the LORD are on the righteous, and
His ears are open to their prayers.
1 PETER 3:12

Do you have a good friend? You probably enjoy sharing your favorite fun activities and talking things over with that person. But if you were always too busy to be with your friend, what kind of friend would you be?

Many people who say they love God don't want to spend time with Him. Sometimes they even say they are too busy. But God says to us, "Come with me by yourselves to a quiet place" (Mark 6:31 NIV).

The Bible says that Jesus woke up "a long while before daylight, . . . went out and departed to a solitary place; and there He prayed" (Mark 1:35). If the Son of God needed time alone with His Father, how much more do we?

It's not always easy to take a few minutes to be by yourself and spend time in God's Word and prayer. But it's important to do that if you want a good friendship with God and if you want strength for the problems you face.

Why not begin now to spend time alone with God every day?

OUR STUBBORN WILLS

You must change your hearts and lives! Come back
to God, and he will forgive your sins.

ACTS 3:19 ICB

In new situations, a donkey's instinct is to stand still. If what the donkey is being asked to do doesn't seem good to the donkey, it just won't move. It is *stubborn*—even when someone might be leading it to food or water!

Becoming a Christian is a once-for-all event when we repent of our sins and put our faith in Jesus for salvation. God takes us "out of darkness into His marvelous light" (1 Peter 2:9). But *being* a Christian is a daily experience of turning from sin and living for Jesus through the power of the Holy Spirit. This is where our wills—our desires—come in. Although we have put our faith in Jesus and God has come to live in us, our old human nature is still "alive and kicking." Sometimes we stubbornly want to put ourselves first instead of Jesus. We think we know what is good and don't trust that what Jesus says is best.

It isn't easy to tell your stubborn will to do what Jesus says instead of what you want, but the Holy Spirit will help you do it. Wouldn't you rather obey Jesus than be stubborn like a donkey? He loves you and will lead you to good things.

SEPTEMBER 3

WE NEED MERCY

The LORD is good; His mercy is everlasting.
PSALM 100:5

Sometimes a person convicted of a crime receives a pardon. Even though the person was guilty of the crime, he doesn't have to pay the penalty. The person receives mercy. How do you think you would feel if you received a pardon for a crime? Would you want to commit that crime again? No. You would be grateful to the person who forgave you.

All Christians have been pardoned! God Himself shows us mercy. Even though we are guilty of sin, we don't have to pay the penalty, because Jesus did that for us.

Some people think only about God's love and not about His judgment. But the Bible tells us, "He who does not believe has been judged already" (John 3:18 NASB).

Don't take sin lightly. Don't just say, "Oh well, God will forgive me anyway." God forgives us because of His mercy, but that's not an excuse to sin as much as we want. Instead, God's kindness and mercy should make us want to stop sinning.

God has mercy on us when we repent, but He is also the judge. So repent, and believe in Jesus!

GOD IS IN CONTROL

There is laid up for me the crown of righteousness.

2 TIMOTHY 4:8

Sometimes things happen that we just don't understand. We wonder why people suffer and we might ask, "Where is God? Why did He let that happen? Why doesn't He fix this?"

But if we read the Bible, we see that God is always working out His unchanging plan and purpose for those who love Him.

What is that purpose? One Bible verse says it is to "gather together in one all things in Christ, both which are in heaven and which are on earth" (Ephesians 1:10). Someday all the sin and trouble in this universe will be destroyed, and God's kingdom of righteousness and peace will rule forever.

We can't always see or understand what God is doing. But even when His ways are mysterious, He is always taking care of us, and because He is God, He is always in charge.

So don't be troubled by events in the news. God is always good, and He understands what is best.

SEPTEMBER 5

HOME AT LAST

"Behold, I make all things new."
REVELATION 21:5

What is the most beautiful sight you have ever seen?

Artists try to paint pictures of Heaven, but even their best paintings can't show us Heaven's true beauty. God gave the apostle John a vision of Heaven, and John tried to write about the splendor he saw, but he could only give us hints.

John wrote that the holy city shone "with the glory of God, and its brilliance was like that of a very precious jewel, like a jasper, clear as crystal" (Revelation 21:11 NIV).

The Bible tells us more about Heaven's joy than Heaven's beauty. Heaven will be a happy home because there won't be anything there to spoil happiness. "Nothing evil will be allowed to enter. . . . No longer will there be a curse upon anything. For the throne of God and of the Lamb will be there" (Revelation 21:27; 22:3 NLT).

Our world was perfect when God made it. Sin spoiled God's beautiful world, but God sent Jesus to overcome sin. In Heaven everything will be beautiful and perfect once again—forever!

COMPASSION AND LOVE

Beloved, if God so loved us, we also ought to love one another.

1 JOHN 4:11

Sometimes we look at others whose lives are full of sin and think we are better people than they are. When that happens, we have forgotten how much we have been forgiven!

God, our Father, has shown us such great kindness and gentle mercy. I pray that we will always reach out to lost people to bring them gently to Jesus, with compassion and love in our hearts. Jesus, "when He saw the multitudes, . . . was moved with compassion for them, because they were weary and scattered, like sheep having no shepherd" (Matthew 9:36).

Let me share these lines from an unknown poet:

Just to be tender, just to be true,
Just to be glad the whole day through,
Just to be merciful, just to be mild,
Just to be trustful as a child,
Just to be gentle and kind and sweet,
Just to be helpful with willing feet, . . .
Just to let love be our daily key,
That is God's will for you and me.

Because God loves us, we love one another.

SEPTEMBER 7

GOD HATES SIN

I acknowledged my sin to You, and my iniquity I have not hidden.
PSALM 32:5

When you are with your friends, what do you talk about? Maybe school, or sports, or music? Probably one thing you don't talk about is sin. Sin isn't a popular subject or even a word most people use anymore. Some people don't believe sin exists.

Sin means "to miss the mark." When we don't do things God says are good, and when we do things God says are wrong, we are sinning. God hates sin. Why? Because He loves us, and He knows how sin affects us. Sin hurts us in so many ways, and it separates us from God forever, unless we turn to Jesus as our Savior.

God's views on the subject of sin have never changed. But many people think that God doesn't really mind when they break His commandments and that God doesn't actually hate anything. The image many people have of Him is a kind old grandfather who shakes his head in amusement when his grandchildren misbehave.

But sin is like a deadly cancer that brings pain and death. Never be afraid to confess your sins to God. Don't wait. Receive God's forgiveness so you can be useful to Him and enjoy His love forever.

I SURRENDER

"Whoever desires to come after Me, let him deny himself."
MARK 8:34

Have you ever promised one thing and then done something else? Maybe you told your parents you would come straight home after school, but then you stopped at a friend's house to play video games instead.

Saying one thing and acting another way is called *being double-minded*. If you are double-minded, you aren't showing others a good example of Jesus' love. The Bible says, "A double minded man is unstable in all his ways" (James 1:8 KJV).

How do we stop being double-minded? We decide that we want God's will more than we want our own. Then we aren't pulled in two directions any longer. We surrender our desires and put God's desires first. We are going just one way—God's way.

When you put God's will first in your life, people notice. When you are thankful, serve others, refuse to fight, and are humble instead of proud, others can see Jesus in you. Putting God first changes everything!

Is anything keeping you from surrendering your life to the King of kings and the Lord of lords?

PEACE IN THE STORM

May the God of hope fill you with all joy and peace.
ROMANS 15:13

Thunderstorms, tornadoes, blizzards—bad weather comes in different forms. We don't all experience the same kinds of storms, but everyone's weather includes some.

This is true in life too. We don't all face the same kinds of problems, but everyone's life includes some. And problems are often called storms. We have personal problems, like a friend who is mad at us, or a family member who is sick. We hear about problems in the world around us. But we face other kinds of storms, too, such as storms of being selfish or storms of putting things before Jesus. Storms make us feel unsettled.

A wonderful hymn says, "He gives us peace in the midst of a storm." Do you remember the violent storm that came upon Jesus and His disciples one night on the Sea of Galilee? His disciples were terrified—but Jesus stayed fast asleep. He was at peace because He knew God was in control. He was at peace also because He was the Ruler over the storm, and He knew it would stop at His command: "Peace, be still!" (Mark 4:39).

God's Word still calms the problems in our lives. Is some storm making you fearful today? Stay close to Jesus. His Word brings peace!

REACH FOR GOD'S HAND

The LORD, He is the One who goes before you. He will be with you.

DEUTERONOMY 31:8

Once many years ago when I was going through a hard time, I prayed and prayed, but I felt as though God had disappeared and that I was alone with my problem. Every day felt like a dark night.

I told my mother about this, and I will never forget her reply: "Son, there are many times when God withdraws to test your faith. He wants you to trust Him in the darkness. Now, Son, reach up by faith in the fog, and you will find that His hand will be there."

I followed my mother's advice. In tears I knelt by my bed, and I experienced a powerful sense of God's presence.

Whether or not we feel God's presence when our way seems dark, by faith we know He is there! When you can't tell how He is leading or working in your life, keep trusting Him and turning to Him. God's love for you is unending and greater than you can imagine! You can build your life on His promise: "I will never leave you nor forsake you" (Hebrews 13:5).

SEPTEMBER 11

THINGS THAT CANNOT BE SHAKEN

We are receiving a kingdom which cannot be shaken.
HEBREWS 12:28

The date of September 11 is remembered by people everywhere and will be for generations to come. On that terrible day in 2001, four passenger jets were hijacked and used as weapons against the United States. Two planes hit the towers of the World Trade Center in New York City, one struck the Pentagon just outside Washington, D.C., and the fourth crashed in a Pennsylvania field. Thousands of innocent people died.

What does God want us to learn from tragedies like 9/11? I confess I don't know the full answer. I know it caused many people to turn to God for the first time, and millions came together to pray.

But one lesson God would teach us all is this: our only lasting hope is in Him. Life has always been uncertain, and events like 9/11 only make that clearer. Only God's kingdom will never end. Put your life in Jesus' hands, for He alone offers us "a kingdom which cannot be shaken."

ANGELS WATCHING

We should live soberly, righteously, and godly in the present age.

TITUS 2:12

I f you have older brothers or sisters, you probably look up to them and want to do what they do. If you are the oldest child in your family, you might have younger brothers or sisters who like to follow you around. Sometimes we think it doesn't matter what we do because no one is watching. But that's not true. Others watch and learn from us.

And God's angels are watching too. The apostle Paul wrote to young Timothy, "I solemnly charge you in the presence of God and of Christ Jesus and of His chosen angels that you guard and keep these rules" (1 Timothy 5:21 AMP).

Think of it: even the angels of Heaven are constantly watching how we live as Christians! They aren't just curious—they know that what we do is important. They want our lives to give God glory.

Don't think it doesn't matter how you live. It does! It matters to God, and it matters to His holy angels. It also matters to those around you. Jesus said, "Let your light so shine before men, that they may see your good works and glorify your Father in heaven" (Matthew 5:16).

SEPTEMBER 13

ABUNDANT PARDON

Blessed is he whose transgression is forgiven, whose sin is covered.
PSALM 32:1

The story is told about a young man in the eighteenth century who joined the British army, but when the shots began to fly, he ran away. Years later he became a great astronomer and discovered the planet Uranus. King George sent for him. He came, fearful the king would order his execution for running away from battle. But he was given an envelope—and inside was a royal pardon. The king said, "Now we can talk, and you shall come up and live at Windsor Castle." He was Sir William Herschel.

Herschel was guilty and deserved condemnation. But King George had mercy on him, and even made him a member of the royal household. This is what God promises us. We are guilty and helpless. But God loves us, and "he saved us, not because of righteous things we had done, but because of his mercy" (Titus 3:5 NIV). Never forget: "God did not send His Son into the world to condemn the world, but that the world through Him might be saved" (John 3:17).

ENJOYING, NOT ABUSING

Do not love the world or the things in the world.
1 JOHN 2:15

No more candy. You'll spoil your dinner." "That's all the TV for today—it's time to do homework." Have you heard statements like these? Adults want you to balance things like candy and TV time with more important things, like a healthy meal and getting your homework done.

Some things, like candy and TV, aren't sinful in themselves; they only become sinful if they are abused. Pleasure isn't wrong—unless it is abused, for example, by overeating. Ambition isn't wrong—unless it is abused, for example, by cheating on a test.

The Bible says, "Do not love the world or the things in the world." This does not mean we can't enjoy the good things God created for us. It is a warning not to be worldly. Worldliness is an attitude that puts *you* first and ignores God and His commandments. Worldly people abuse God's good gifts. They care only about their own lives on earth, not about eternity.

Don't let a spirit of worldliness creep into your life. Ask God to help you follow Him and His ways today.

GOD VALUES FAITH

How precious also are Your thoughts to me,
O God! How great is the sum of them!
PSALM 139:17

Have you ever watched a nest of baby birds being fed by their parents? Those baby birds trust that they will be fed, and they open up their mouths wide in anticipation.

All through the Bible we learn how much it pleases God when we trust Him for everything we need. The Roman soldier expressed great faith when he told Jesus just to "say the word" (Luke 7:7) and his servant would be healed. Jesus told His disciples, "Look at the birds . . . they neither sow nor reap nor gather into barns; yet your heavenly Father feeds them. Are you not of more value than they?" (Matthew 6:26).

How do we develop trust? By spending time in God's presence. As we pray, worship, and read His Word, we get to know God better. We learn what He is like. We see how much He cares about us and that He always keeps His promises. We develop trust also as we step out in faith, do what He says, and discover He really can be trusted.

God values our trust in Him. Are you trusting Him for every need in your life today?

DON'T SINK!

This is how we know that he lives in us: We
know it by the Spirit he gave us.
1 JOHN 3:24 NIV

A boat doesn't sink because it is in the water. It sinks when water gets into it!

In the same way, we don't fail to live as we should because we are in the world. We fail because the world has gotten into us.

It can happen almost without us realizing it. At one time we were living for Jesus, surrendering our wills to the will of God. But little by little the chilling "waters" of the world crept into our "boats." We became much more concerned about the things of this world than the things Jesus says are important.

Most ocean-going ships have pumps running constantly, sucking out any water that might have crept into the ship. Like those ships, we need to keep "pumps" running by asking God to forgive our sins. We need to "plug the holes" with the truth of God's Word. God is with us, and His Spirit will help us and keep us strong if we ask.

Have you been thinking more lately about clothes, sports, and popularity than about pleasing God? Don't let the world sink your ship!

SEPTEMBER 17

PERFECT PEACE

May the God of hope fill you with all joy and peace.
ROMANS 15:13

Some railroad workers found a bird's nest under some train tracks. In the nest a bird sat peacefully on her eggs, undisturbed by the roar of the fast trains above and around her. What a picture of perfect trust! The Bible says, "You will keep him in perfect peace, whose mind is stayed on You" (Isaiah 26:3).

I know that growing up brings challenges, but you never need to doubt that God will give you the help and strength you need to face them. Quietly trust that God is still in charge and working out things according to His own good plan. Believe me, God's grace is more than enough for this time of your life. Even as I grow older, I am learning, day by day, to keep my mind focused on Jesus. When I do, the worries and anxieties and concerns of the world pass away, and nothing but "perfect peace" is left in my heart.

Always remember Jesus, what He has done for you and how much He loves you. Then you will have His joy and peace in your heart too.

PRAY CONTINUALLY

Men always ought to pray and not lose heart.

LUKE 18:1

My wife kept a notebook with the things our children said as they were beginning to talk. She treasured these first attempts, mistakes and all.

God feels the same way about your prayers. A prayer doesn't need special words. Sometimes people feel uncomfortable or shy when they first learn to pray, and that's fine. It's important just to begin. In fact, sometimes our simplest, most heartfelt prayers are the most pleasing to God.

When Paul said we should "pray continually" (1 Thessalonians 5:17 NIV), he chose a term used to describe a cough that doesn't go away. He meant that over and over throughout our day, we should turn quickly to God to praise and thank Him, and to ask for His help. God is interested in everything we do, and nothing is too big or too small to talk over with Him.

When you made the decision to follow Jesus, you became a child of God, adopted into His family forever. Now you have the wonderful privilege of coming right into His presence and calling Him "Father" when you pray.

God encourages us when we pray. What do you want to pray about right now?

JESUS IS COMING AGAIN

Looking for the blessed hope and glorious
appearing of our . . . Savior Jesus Christ.
TITUS 2:13

D o you ever feel discouraged? One of the best ways to get rid of discouragement is to remember that Jesus is coming again. What is happening in your life right now is not going to last forever!

The most thrilling, glorious truth in all the world is the second coming of Jesus. When you hear about scary events and people talk like there's no hope, remember that the Bible is the only book in the world that truthfully tells us about the future. The Bible is more modern than tomorrow's news alert, and it says Jesus is coming again.

This truth gives us hope—but it should also make us more caring and more motivated to tell others about Jesus. After all, we don't know when Jesus will return. He said Himself, "Of that day and hour no one knows, not even the angels of heaven, but My Father only" (Matthew 24:36).

Believing that Jesus is coming back doesn't make us less concerned about this world. It makes us *more* concerned, because we know it could be any day. *Now* is the time to live for Jesus and help other people know Him too.

CHOOSE GOD'S WORD

Your word I have hidden in my heart, that I might not sin against You.

PSALM 119:11

D o you have any favorite Bible verses or stories?

The Bible isn't just another great book. It is God's Word, given by God to tell us about Himself. I have known many outstanding leaders who made the Bible their guide. One successful businessman told me he began each day by reading the Sermon on the Mount aloud.

The Bible tells us how it came to be written. In one of his letters, the apostle Peter wrote, "We did not follow cunningly devised fables . . . for prophecy never came by the will of man, but holy men of God spoke as they were moved by the Holy Spirit" (2 Peter 1:16, 21). The apostle Paul wrote, "All Scripture is given by inspiration of God, and is profitable for doctrine, for reproof, for correction, for instruction in righteousness" (2 Timothy 3:16).

As you get to know the Bible, you get to know God. Don't get too busy to have time to read the Bible. Many years ago I heard these words: "Sin will keep you from God's Word—or God's Word will keep you from sin!" Which will you choose today?

GOD OF ALL COMFORT

Because he himself suffered when he was tempted, he
is able to help those who are being tempted.
HEBREWS 2:18 NIV

Once when I was in my late teens, I was in love with a girl. It might
have been just "puppy love," but it was real to me, the puppy! We
planned to be married, even though we were both much too young. But
then she felt the Lord was leading her to marry a different young man—
one of my best friends!

I had a broken heart. I visited a friend who was a minister to seek
his help. He turned me to 2 Corinthians 1:3–4: "Blessed be the God and
Father of our Lord Jesus Christ . . . who comforts us in all our tribulation,
that we may be able to comfort those who are in any trouble, with the
comfort with which we ourselves are comforted by God." Not only did
these words comfort me, but I learned something about problems. I
learned that my experiences could encourage and comfort other people.

Has God taught you something that could help someone else today?

SEARCHING FOR HOPE

"In the world you will have tribulation; but be of
good cheer, I have overcome the world."
JOHN 16:33

Once when I spoke to college students about the future God is plan-
ning, a student asked, "Isn't thinking about Heaven just trying to
escape our problems here?"

God promises "new heavens and a new earth in which righteousness dwells" (2 Peter 3:13). But in the meantime, we live each day with
Jesus and make it a good day. No matter what happens around us, today
is a good day to be alive. God is on His throne, He loves us, and we can
look forward to a wonderful future with Him!

Some people think if they become Christians, God will take away all
their problems. It just isn't so. Jesus said, "In the world you will have
tribulation." We still struggle with doing the wrong things, and Satan is
still at work.

But that isn't the full story! Jesus added, "But be of good cheer, I
have overcome the world." He not only *will* overcome the world—He
already has!

SEPTEMBER 23

GOD'S WORD

Desire the pure milk of the word, that you may grow thereby.
1 PETER 2:2

We all need spiritual food, just as our bodies need physical food. Where do we find this spiritual food? In the Bible, the Word of God. The Bible shows us Jesus, the Bread of Life and the Water of Life. If we fail to partake of this spiritual nourishment, we will lose our spiritual health.

Some Christians do not have the same freedom we have to read the Bible. In some parts of the world, owning a Bible is against the law. There are many Christians in the world who are too poor to own a Bible. And some other people don't have the Bible in their own language yet. But most of us don't have any of these excuses. Whenever these Christians get to hold and read even a portion of God's Word, they are so grateful. The problem for most of us is not getting a Bible, but using a Bible—actually picking it up and reading it.

Learn to read the Bible well. Don't just skim through it. Think about what you read, and memorize verses, hiding them in your heart. Read the Bible as if your life depended on it—because if you want to keep growing as a believer, it does!

GOD REVEALED

Forever, O LORD, Your word is settled in heaven.

PSALM 119:89

Have you ever discovered that a favorite author of yours had written many more books? You probably couldn't wait to find the other books and read them all! We should have that same excitement about reading the Bible.

The Bible is God's revelation of Himself. What does *revelation* mean? It means that something that once was hidden is now made known. If it isn't revealed, it remains hidden. Some people see God that way—hidden and unknown. But God has revealed Himself. He is not hidden! He is not just some vague force, like gravity. He has spoken to us, and if we will listen, we can discover what He is like, and we can come to know Him in a personal way.

God has two "textbooks." One is the textbook of nature. By looking at the world, we can learn something about the Creator. The other textbook is the Bible. It is so much more than a record of ancient events; it is God's Word. The Bible was given to us by the Holy Spirit to guide our lives.

God has spoken—and He still speaks. Are you listening by reading God's Word?

TREASURE THAT LASTS

"Lay up for yourselves treasures in heaven."
MATTHEW 6:20

Some time ago two old friends were dying. One was rich, and the other poor. The rich man had never accepted Jesus, but the poor man was a strong believer. One day the rich man said to his friend, "When I die, I shall have to leave my riches. When you die, you will go to yours."

The man with everything actually had nothing, and the man with nothing actually had everything.

These two men illustrate what Jesus said to His disciples: "Do not lay up for yourselves treasures on earth, . . . but lay up for yourselves treasures in heaven. . . . For where your treasure is, there your heart will be also" (Matthew 6:19–21).

Does that mean we need to give up everything we own or never spend our allowance on ourselves? No, not unless God clearly commands us. But it does mean we should treat everything we have—including our lives—as if it all belongs to Jesus because, actually, it does.

Will you put His will above everything else today?

SEPTEMBER 26

FAITH IN GOD

Faith is the substance of things hoped for.
HEBREWS 11:1

In English class, you learn about subjects, verbs, and objects. Like some verbs, faith must have an object. We don't simply have faith; we have faith in something or someone.

For the Christian there is only one object for faith: our living God. Our faith is in the God who created this world and came down to earth in the person of His Son, Jesus. We put our faith in Jesus because He alone is the Savior. The Bible says, "Through Him [you] believe in God, who raised Him from the dead and gave Him glory, so that your faith and hope are in God" (1 Peter 1:21).

Listen to your friends and other people around you, and you will realize that many people put their faith in all kinds of ideas and beliefs, from human leaders to science to pride in their own abilities. But only Jesus reveals God to us, and only He can bridge the gap between us and God—the gap caused by sin.

Don't be deceived or misled. Only Jesus is worthy of your faith.

SEPTEMBER 27

OUR GREAT ASSURANCE

Let us draw near with a true heart in full assurance of faith.
HEBREWS 10:22

It's amazing how quickly our feelings can change. One day you can't stop smiling because you got an *A*, and the next day you're down because a friend hurt your feelings. Then before you know it, you're back to feeling on top of the world after you score a winning goal for your team!

It's a good thing that when it comes to being saved, we don't rely on our up-and-down feelings. Only the facts matter—the fact that Jesus died for our sins and rose again, and the fact that if we have given our lives to Him, He has promised to forgive us and save us. The Bible says, "God has given us eternal life, and this life is in His Son. He who has the Son has life" (1 John 5:11–12).

God cannot lie. Your feelings will lie to you—and Satan might even use them to trick you into thinking God has left you all alone. But remember what Jesus said about Satan: "There is no truth in him. . . . He is a liar and the father of lies" (John 8:44 NIV).

How wonderful to know our faith is based on God's truth and not our up-and-down feelings!

TO DIE IS GAIN

To me, to live is Christ and to die is gain.

PHILIPPIANS 1:21 NIV

Have you ever watched a movie and found yourself crying because a character in the story died? Tears are a natural response to death.

Sometimes we ask God why someone died. We loved them, and they loved God. Wouldn't they have done more good if they had lived longer?

Someday, after Jesus comes back, there will be no more death! How wonderful that will be——never to have to say good-bye to those we love. Until then, however, people do die, mostly when they are old. And God knows and cares about the death of His people. The Bible says He sees every sparrow's fall and He sees the number of hairs on our heads, so of course He knows and cares about everything that happens to us.

The apostle Paul wrote, "To me, to live is Christ and to die is gain." This is true for everyone who follows Jesus. Even when we are sad or confused because someone has died, we still can trust God's all-knowing love.

SAFE AND SECURE

He became the author of eternal salvation to all who obey Him.
HEBREWS 5:9

The ark that Noah built was huge, and no one around him had ever seen rain. Can you imagine what his neighbors said? "God is going to judge the world with a flood? Really?!" Can you picture them shaking their heads and laughing, calling Noah a fool and telling him he was out of his mind? Can you hear them angrily rejecting his warnings of coming judgment?

Noah was probably mocked more than anyone else in the Bible, except for Jesus. But he "did everything that God commanded him" (Genesis 6:22 ICB). And when the flood came, only Noah and his family were saved. For those who ignored Noah's pleas, it was too late.

You and I are called to give a message that often seems like foolishness to an unbelieving world—the message of the cross. Will everyone accept it? No. Will some mock us? Yes. But never stop sharing the gospel, because it is still "the power of God for the salvation of everyone who believes" (Romans 1:16 NIV).

DISPEL DISCOURAGEMENT

Wait on the LORD; be of good courage, and He shall strengthen your heart.

PSALM 27:14

In the classic book and movie *Pollyanna*, a young orphan encourages herself and others by playing the Glad Game—always finding something to be glad about in every situation. Eventually Pollyanna's cheerful attitude is tested when she can't walk after a serious accident.

When have you felt discouraged? Maybe you've been injured, or you're having trouble with math at school. Maybe someone you care about is sick, or you're always on the bench when your team plays. Even though we can often find something to be glad about in every situation, everyone does feel discouraged at times.

Discouragement is like a cloud that blocks out the light and warmth of the sun. When we are discouraged, we can't see God at work in our lives.

There is only one way to get rid of discouragement, and it is not in our own strength or effort. We need to turn in faith to God, believing that He loves us and is in control of the future. The Bible says, "Wait on the Lord . . . and He shall strengthen your heart."

OCTOBER

Neither death nor life, . . . nor things present nor things to
come, . . . shall be able to separate us from the love of God.
ROMANS 8:38–39

GOOD AND BAD

Every good gift and every perfect gift is from above,
and comes down from the Father of lights.
JAMES 1:17

D o you ever wonder why bad things happen?

Death and pain and every other tragedy came into the world because of sin. When Adam and Eve sinned in the garden of Eden, they weren't just doing something God had told them not to do. They were turning against God in their thoughts, words, and actions.

God had made them and provided everything they needed, but they decided to believe Satan's lie instead of obeying God. Satan's lie was that eating the fruit would make them "be like God" (Genesis 3:5). Instead, eating the fruit God had told them not to eat brought all kinds of sin and evil into the world.

No, I don't fully understand why God *allows* evil to happen. But someday He will put an end to it. And even though bad things do happen, our world is still full of God's wonderful gifts. Beauty, love, music, and friendship are just some of God's good gifts. Can you name some of God's good gifts to you today?

If it had not been for sin, Jesus never would have had to die. But Jesus triumphed over the bad—and so can we, because of Him.

POOR IN SPIRIT

"Where your treasure is, there your heart will be also."

MATTHEW 6:21

When you win a game at an amusement park or festival, you earn a prize, or you collect tickets and turn them in to pick out the prize you have earned.

One of the hardest truths for people to accept is that there is absolutely nothing we can do to *earn* salvation. No matter how generous, honest, good, or compassionate we are—it can never be enough. God is holy and perfect. If we think we are good enough to live with Him in Heaven forever, that simply points out our sinful pride.

When we see ourselves as God sees us—as sinners—*then* we realize our need of a Savior. But the amazing thing is this: God still loves us even though we are sinners! He loves us so much that Jesus died on the cross for us.

All we can do is believe and receive—believe Jesus died for us and by faith receive Him into our lives. Don't depend on your own goodness. Instead, treasure what Jesus did for you to make it possible for you to be forgiven.

No, we can't earn our salvation. But Jesus won it for us—on the cross!

OCTOBER 3

ANSWERED PRAYER

Let us . . . approach the throne of grace with
confidence, so that we may receive mercy.
HEBREWS 4:16 NIV

oes God answer your prayers? Yes, always.

Frequently people say to me, "God answered my prayer!"
Usually they mean God gave them whatever they had asked for, either
for themselves or for others.

But God always answers the prayers of His children. His answer isn't
always "yes," however. Sometimes His answer is "no" or "wait"—and
those are answers just as much as "yes."

Think about the apostle Paul, who asked God three times to remove
a painful problem (probably an illness of some kind). But God's answer
was no (2 Corinthians 12:7–10). God had something better for Paul—a
path leading him into deeper dependence on God and His grace. And
think about Jesus and His prayer before He faced the cross: "If it is
possible, let this cup of suffering be taken away from me" (Matthew
26:39 NLT). But God's answer was "no"—because there was no other
way for our salvation to be won.

God knows far better than we do what is best for us. We can thank
Him even when He says "no" or "wait." His answer is always perfect.

GOD'S PLANS ARE BEST

As for God, His way is perfect.

PSALM 18:30

You might have planned an outdoor picnic, but the weather turned rainy and cold. You might have planned to go to your best friend's birthday party, but you came down with a stomach bug. Things don't always work out the way we plan. That's how it was for the apostle Paul too.

Paul expected to preach in Asia Minor, but he was "forbidden by the Holy Spirit" (Acts 16:6). He looked forward to teaching the new Christians in Philippi, but he wound up thrown into prison instead (Acts 16:11–40). He shared the gospel in Thessalonica, and then a mob suddenly accused him of turning the world upside down and forced him to flee for his life (Acts 17:6–10).

But God was in control! Paul was forbidden to preach in Asia Minor—because God was opening the door to Europe. Paul found himself in jail, and the jailer and his family became believers. Paul left Thessalonica, and the next town, Berea, "received the word with all readiness" (Acts 17:11).

Things don't always work out the way we plan. But if we commit our way to Jesus and walk in obedience to Him, we discover His plans are always better.

NO OTHER GODS

"You cannot serve both God and Money."
LUKE 16:13 NIV

Have you ever tried to be involved in two activities at the same time? Maybe you played on a basketball team and sang in a choir. If two practices were scheduled at the same time, what did you do? You had to choose.

It's very hard—impossible, really—to give all our time and attention to two things at once. One will win out over the other. This is one reason why the Bible forbids worshiping idols. Almost anything can become an idol—something we worship and serve in place of God. Good grades, the right game, a high-paying job, success in sports—these things aren't necessarily wrong in themselves, but they become idols when we make them the most important things in life.

Idols are false. They can't save us or change our lives for the better. And idols cut us off from God. We substitute them for God—and as a result, we turn our backs on Him and never come to know Him and love Him as we should.

Don't let anything become an idol in your life. God has commanded, "You shall have no other gods before Me" (Exodus 20:3).

STRANGERS IN THE WORLD

I urge you, as aliens and strangers in the
world, to abstain from sinful desires.

1 PETER 2:11 NIV

D o you have any friends who came to this country from another one?
People become immigrants and citizens of a new country because
they are looking for a better life. Sometimes immigrants fit into their new
communities right away, but other times they are rejected. It might be
hard for them to get a job, or learn the language, or accept new customs.

The Bible says that we are "aliens and strangers in the world." Our
citizenship is in Heaven—that's where our real home is. As long as we
live on this earth, we don't quite fit in. Our customs are different, our
goals are different, our ways of living are different, and our concerns
are different.

And so people may make fun of us because we follow Jesus. They
may reject us and even be mean to us. If this happens to us, we shouldn't
be surprised. Jesus warned us, "If they persecuted Me, they will also
persecute you" (John 15:20).

But never forget: you are a citizen of the kingdom of God. And
someday you will be home!

OCTOBER 7

YIELDED TO GOD

When you offer yourselves to someone to obey him as
slaves, you are slaves to the one whom you obey.
ROMANS 6:16 NIV

Eric Liddell, a missionary to China and an Olympic runner, was competitive and determined to use his abilities to the fullest. But his meekness, kindness, and gentle spirit won admiration even from people he defeated. He was described as "ridiculously humble in victory" and "utterly generous in defeat." That's a good definition of what it means to be meek.

Meekness involves being yielded. The word *yield* has two meanings. It can mean to let go or surrender. Eric Liddell let go of pride whenever he won a race. It can also mean to give. Liddell gave honor and respect to anyone who beat him in a race.

Jesus expressed this idea when He said, "He who loses [or surrenders] his life . . . will find it" (Matthew 10:39). Surrender your will to Jesus' will for you—let go of what you want, and give yourself to God and whatever He wants for you. Then He will give back to you a more wonderful life than anything you could have ever imagined!

GOD'S MESSAGE

"He who hears My word, and believes Him who sent Me, has eternal life."

JOHN 5:24 NASB

I know little about outer space or the creatures living deep in the ocean. Yet I believe they exist. Why? The answer is obvious. Other people study outer space and deep sea life. They have actually been to these places! I read and listen to what they say, and I accept it as the evidence of reliable witnesses.

I spend much of my time with one special book—the Bible. In it I discover that centuries ago God acted and spoke, and reliable witnesses wrote down what they saw and heard. God even guided them as they wrote, so that when I read the Bible now, I read the very words of God Himself!

I may not understand everything there is to know about God—but I know Him and trust Him, because I read of Him in the Bible. Most of all, I know He came down to this earth in the Person of His Son, that "grace and truth came through Jesus" (John 1:17), and through believing in Him, we have eternal life!

OCTOBER 9

A CHEERFUL HEART

You shall surround me with songs of deliverance.
PSALM 32:7

A nineteenth-century German missionary named George Müller
proved over and over again that when faith is strong, troubles
become trifles—small things.

When George decided to become a missionary, his father refused to
pay for his schooling. George asked God to provide the money, and soon
someone offered him a tutoring job. Later, George built an orphanage
for three hundred children. All the building supplies and provisions for
the orphans came in answer to George's faith and prayers!

Faith does makes our problems smaller, but that doesn't mean our
troubles aren't real or that we should act as if they don't exist. God takes
them seriously—so seriously that He sent Jesus into the world to deal
with the root cause of everyone's problems, which is sin.

Just as Jesus overcame death, He helps us overcome trouble. "I will
turn their mourning to joy" (Jeremiah 31:13), the Bible says. Even in the
middle of problems, He can give us hope and deliver us.

How does that happen? We look in faith to God. He never leaves us,
and He has plans for our future. He can even give us a cheerful heart
and a smile to match our faith!

THE CLOUDS OF LIFE

The Lord went before them by day in a pillar of cloud to lead the way.

EXODUS 13:21

Meteorologists study earth's atmosphere and predict the weather. One thing they watch is the types of clouds in the sky. Certain kinds of clouds are a clue about the weather that is coming.

The Israelites in the wilderness followed a cloud—but not an ordinary one. As they traveled to the promised land, the Bible says, "The Lord went before them by day in a pillar of cloud to lead the way."

Like the Israelites, we also are travelers. As we go through life, we need a guide to show us the way. At times we'll have problems and feel as if we are going through a wilderness. Whatever our situation, God is with us, and He goes before us to encourage and guide us.

God brought the Israelites through the wilderness—and He will bring you through everything in your life as you look in faith to Him. Never forget: "He is the living God, and steadfast forever" (Daniel 6:26).

REDEEMED BY LOVE

You were redeemed . . . with the precious blood of Christ.
1 PETER 1:18–19 NIV

The word *redeem* means to "buy back"—to get something back by paying a price. To be redeemed can be illustrated like this: Suppose you had a beloved family dog, but the dog ran away, and another family took him in. Eventually you found your dog, but the other family wouldn't give him back to you, so you *paid* the other family a lot of money and bought your dog back from them. You *redeemed* your dog at great personal cost because you loved and valued him.

That is a picture of what God did for us. Adam and Eve left God's family and were taken in by Satan. All humanity became slaves of sin with no hope of deliverance. But God still loved us, and He had already determined how He would bring us back to His household.

By dying on the cross, Jesus paid the price to buy us back with His own blood, a price far greater than our true value. He did it solely because He loved us. Now we have been redeemed!

DETERMINED DISCIPLES

"If you hold to my teaching, you are really my disciples."

JOHN 8:31 NIV

Have you ever had a flower or vegetable garden? Good soil, water, and sunshine keep a plant healthy and growing strong. But what happens to part of the plant that gets broken off the vine? Yes, it wilts, withers, and dies.

All of us who belong to Christ are called to be *disciples*. A disciple in Jesus' time was someone who followed a particular teacher. A disciple was both a learner and a follower—believing the teacher's message and then putting it into practice.

Unlike the original disciples, we can't physically spend time with Jesus, but we can learn from Him by reading His Word and doing what He says there. This is how we stay connected to the vine and grow healthy and strong in spirit.

Jesus gave the word *disciple* an extra meaning too. He sent His disciples out to tell others about Him. So disciples of Jesus are people who have committed their lives to Jesus and seek each day to learn, to follow, and to share Him with others. Does this describe you? Stay connected to the vine today!

OCTOBER 13

TRUE CHANGE

Return to the LORD your God, for He is gracious and merciful.
JOEL 2:13

From time to time, people have talked to me about their biggest
problems because their sins had been discovered and they were in
serious trouble. They wept bitterly because they had lost their business
or hurt their marriage or ruined their reputation.

But later I would hear that they were back in the same situation.
They had not learned from their experience. They had not changed at all,
and even seemed determined to bring more heartache into their lives.

Why? Their tears were tears of self-pity and not of repentance. True
repentance is turning away from sin—a conscious, deliberate decision
to leave sin behind—and then consciously turning to God, with a commitment to follow His will.

Repentance is only one part of our response to Jesus (and even
the strength to repent comes from God). But if we do not repent—
turn from sin—we can't claim Jesus is our Lord. The Bible says, "Godly
sorrow brings repentance that leads to salvation and leaves no regret"
(2 Corinthians 7:10 NIV). We don't have to live with regret.

WE CAN TRUST GOD

Neither death nor life, . . . nor things present nor things to
come, . . . shall be able to separate us from the love of God.
ROMANS 8:38—39

Some days it seems like nothing goes right. We run into problems at
home and at school, and we hear about problems in the world. How
do you respond on days like that?

There are two ways to respond: discouragement or trust.

The problem with giving in to discouragement is that it only makes
things worse. Discouragement opens the door to other negative emotions, like anger or jealousy. Sometimes people even try to escape
through drugs or alcohol. But do any of these solve the problem? No!

God has a better way—the way of trust. Sometimes He might show
us that we were in the wrong. Other times we can only accept what is
happening and ask God to help us go through it.

One of the best ways to overcome hardship, I've found, is to praise
God right in the middle of it! Turning to God's Word encourages us too.
Many of the psalms, for example, were written by someone who was
suffering.

Today, follow the example of King David, who wrote, "Bless the Lord,
O my soul, and forget not all His benefits" (Psalm 103:2). God is always
with you. Nothing can separate you from Him!

UPSIDE DOWN OR RIGHT SIDE UP?

God is not ashamed to be called their God.
HEBREWS 11:16

We live in an upside-down world. People hate when they should love, quarrel when they should be friendly, fight when they should be peaceful, wound when they should heal, steal when they should share, and do wrong when they should do right.

I once saw a toy clown with a weight in its head. No matter how it was placed, it invariably assumed an upside-down position. Whether someone set it on its feet or on its side, when they let go, the little clown flipped back over onto its head.

The toy clown shows us why Jesus' disciples seemed to be misfits to the world. Christians are right-side-up people in an upside-down world—where right-side-up people seem upside down. To unbelievers, the true Christian seems odd and not normal at all.

Yet all around us are people who sense something is wrong with their topsy-turvy lives, and they yearn to be right side up. Will you pray for them and ask God to help you point them to Jesus?

HOPE FROM GOD'S WORD

The grass withers, the flower fades, but the
word of our God stands forever.
ISAIAH 40:8

A missionary in China, imprisoned during World War II, managed to take a copy of the gospel of John with her into prison. She carefully hid it, and each night when she went to bed, she pulled the covers over her head and memorized one verse. She did this until the day she was freed.

When the prisoners were released, most were weak and downcast, but the missionary was so upbeat someone said she must have been brainwashed. A reporter who interviewed her said, "She's been brainwashed for sure. God washed her brain."

I want to encourage you not only to read God's Word but also to memorize it. You might think it would be too hard, but remember how easily you memorize a new song or a TV commercial. As you repeat a verse or a group of verses over and over, you will find they begin to take root in your soul. Then when you need them, those verses will come to mind and give you help and hope. The psalmist declared, "Your word I have hidden in my heart, that I might not sin against You" (Psalm 119:11).

Are you storing up God's Word in your heart and mind? If not, begin today!

LOVE AND MARRIAGE

He who loves his wife loves himself.
EPHESIANS 5:28

It will be quite a few years before you are ready to get married! But while you are young, it's good to think about what makes a marriage strong and what you will look for in a husband or a wife.

There are three "ingredients" that make a successful marriage. The first is love—not just an emotional feeling or a physical attraction, but a deep commitment to put the other person first. The apostle Paul defined love beautifully in 1 Corinthians 13. Read it and you will know how God defines love.

Maturity is the second ingredient. *Maturity* means a willingness to act responsibly and not take the easy way out. Mature people are willing to listen to each other and make decisions that will be good for both of them.

The third ingredient is faith. Marriage is wonderful, but not always easy. Without Jesus at the center of a marriage and a home, it becomes even more difficult. But with Jesus—with His presence and His Word, with prayer and faith—a husband and wife can deal with every problem.

So remember, it takes these three ingredients plus three people to make a great marriage: you, your husband or wife, and Jesus.

WANTED!

Come near to God and he will come near to you.

JAMES 4:8 NIV

Parents look forward to the birth of their baby—they can hardly wait to hold that little one in their arms. Adoptive parents wait anxiously for the day a judge declares their adopted child to be their own. Foster parents gladly welcome children into their home. All kinds of parents love their children and want to be with them.

It is the same with God and His children. The Bible says, "Come near to God and he will come near to you." What a wonderful promise this is! It means each of us can come close to God, knowing He will come close to us—because He wants to be with us!

But sometimes we have too many distractions, and we don't take time to be alone with God. School, sports, homework, television, the Internet, friends, and even church activities take up our time, while the most important thing we could do goes undone.

Maybe we will have to change our priorities. Maybe we will have to say no to some activities. Whatever it takes, make time to be alone with God.

Remember: He will come near to you, if you will come near to Him.

TEACHER AND GUIDE

"When He, the Spirit of truth, has come, He will guide you into all truth."
JOHN 16:13

Do you have a favorite teacher? Good teachers guide their students to learn and enjoy learning. Did you know that all Christians have the same teacher? The moment we receive Jesus as Savior and Lord, the Holy Spirit comes to live inside us! The Bible says, "If anyone does not have the Spirit of Christ, he is not His" (Romans 8:9).

The Holy Spirit helps us in life's ups and downs, and He has two other important roles in our lives. First, He convicts us of sin. He helps us see where we are wrong. The Bible says, "He will convict the world of sin, and of righteousness, and of judgment" (John 16:8). This verse focuses on the Holy Spirit's power among unbelievers, but He also makes believers aware when we sin.

The second role of the Holy Spirit is teacher. The Bible says, "He will guide you into all truth." Just as surely as the Holy Spirit inspired the writers of the Bible, He instructs us as we read and think on God's Word.

Are you a willing student of the Holy Spirit? He is the best Teacher you will ever have!

MOVED WITH COMPASSION

You, O Lord, are a God full of compassion, . . .
abundant in mercy and truth.
PSALM 86:15

In Australia, a horse became trapped in mud on a beach, unable to move, and the tide was coming in. For three hours a woman held the horse's head up above the rising water so it would not drown. The horse's life was saved because of the woman's concern and compassion.

The word *compassion* comes from two Latin words meaning "to suffer with." What better picture to describe God's compassion for us?

You might see pictures of people suffering because of war or terrible storms or sickness. But all around us are people who suffer with loneliness, fear, sadness, poverty, or a multitude of other problems that we might not be able to see.

But God sees, and He has compassion on us—He suffers with us. He knows what we are going through, and He cares. The greatest act of compassion of all time was when Jesus suffered in our place on the cross.

Now He calls us to have compassion on others, for His sake—to see their need, do what we can to show we care, and point them to the One who suffered for us all. The Bible says, "Be sympathetic, love as brothers, be compassionate and humble" (1 Peter 3:8 NIV).

OCTOBER 21

"COME HOME"

Our citizenship is in heaven, from which we
also eagerly wait for the Savior.
PHILIPPIANS 3:20

Once there was a poor widow and her son who lived in a cheap, run-down attic. Years before, she had married against her parents' wishes and had gone with her husband to live in a foreign land. But he was irresponsible, and after a few years he died, leaving no provision for his wife and child.

One day the mother found a letter in her mailbox. She recognized the handwriting on the envelope, and her fingers trembled as she opened it. Inside was a check and a slip of paper with just two words: "Come home."

It doesn't matter who we are or what we do; someday everyone who knows Jesus will have a similar experience. We don't know when. But when Jesus returns, it will be as if we all received a note with the same message: "Come home." Heaven will be ready for us, and we will get to live there with God forever. What a wonderful day that will be!

IT WAS LOVE

"I have loved you with an everlasting love; therefore
with lovingkindness I have drawn you."
JEREMIAH 31:3

Sometimes people have difficulty believing God is a God of love. They ask, "How could He be, when the world is filled with so much suffering?" If you ever wonder whether God is love, look at the cross. It was love that led Jesus to the cross.

It was love that held Him back when He was falsely accused of blasphemy—disrespecting God—and led Him to Golgotha to die with common thieves. He could have called armies of angels to come to His defense, but it was love that kept Him from raising a hand against His enemies.

It was love that made Him pause, despite His own pain, to give hope to a repentant sinner on a cross beside Him who cried, "Lord, remember me when You come into Your kingdom" (Luke 23:42).

It was love that caused Jesus to lift His voice and pray, "Father, forgive them, for they do not know what they do" (Luke 23:34).

Does God love us? Does He love you? Yes—and the proof is the cross.

A CLEAR CONSCIENCE

The blood of Christ . . . [will] cleanse our consciences.
HEBREWS 9:14 NIV

Have you ever had a favorite shirt that got so badly stained you couldn't wear it anymore? Then you washed it with a special stain-removing product—and the stains were gone! You could wear the shirt again.

Our consciences are like that shirt. Each of us has a conscience that guides and judges everything we think and do. But by itself, a conscience is not a reliable guide. The Bible says that sin has affected our conscience and what we see as right or wrong. Satan can even twist our consciences if they are not yielded to Jesus and convince us that wrong is really right.

Our conscience needs to be cleansed by the Holy Spirit and washed by the truth of the Word of God. Then, like your favorite shirt, it becomes useful again.

Is God speaking to you through your conscience about something that is not right in your life? Something you may be doing but you know does not please Jesus? Are you listening?

RESTING FAITH

The testing of your faith produces patience.
JAMES 1:3

A famous preacher, Dwight L. Moody, was fond of pointing out that there are three kinds of faith in Jesus: First, *struggling faith*, which is like a man floundering and fearful in deep water. Second, *clinging faith*, which is like a man hanging to the side of a boat. Third, *resting faith*, which is like a man safe inside the boat—strong and secure enough to reach out his hand to help someone else.

Notice each man had faith. Each knew the boat was his only hope. But only one had a resting faith. Only one had discovered he could actually be in the boat, where all he had to do was rest.

This is the kind of faith God wants us to have—faith that trusts Him totally. But sometimes we discover resting faith only after we have endured a time of struggling or clinging faith. Sometimes we only realize we can get in the boat when the storm rages and we cry out to God. Then our Savior graciously extends His hand and says, "Come to Me, . . . and I will give you rest" (Matthew 11:28).

Don't be afraid when your faith is tested—you will be rewarded with even stronger faith!

DOING GOD'S WILL

[Do] the will of God from the heart.
EPHESIANS 6:6

Sometimes people think God's will is sure to make them miserable. They think that He will send them someplace they don't want to go or give them work they don't want to do. But the Bible says, "Do not be unwise, but understand what the will of the Lord is" (Ephesians 5:17).

Listen: God's will comes from God's love. If you love people, do you want to make them miserable? Will you go out of your way to punish them if they don't do exactly what you tell them to? No, of course not—not if you really love them.

The same is true with God. God loves you, and because He loves you, He cares what happens to you. He loves you too much to let you wander aimlessly through life, without meaning or purpose. His will for you is to follow Him. The Bible says, "You will show me the path of life; in Your presence is fullness of joy" (Psalm 16:11).

Desire God's will for your life more than anything else. To know God's will—and to do it—is life's greatest joy.

ONE SURE GUIDE

Your word is a lamp to my feet and a light to my path.

PSALM 119:105

I f you are ever lost in the woods, you'll need a compass to find your way out. A map and a flashlight might help too.

Christians have a compass, a map, and a light all in one precious Guide—the Word of God.

The world is full of voices calling us to go this way or that way. But Christians have just one authority, the Bible. It is the only voice that will tell us the truth. God gave us His Word to tell us what to believe and how to live. As the psalmist said, "The teaching of your word gives light, so even the simple can understand" (Psalm 119:130 NLT).

In a letter to a friend, Abraham Lincoln said, "I am profitably engaged in reading the Bible. Take all of this Book upon reason that you can and the balance upon faith, and you will live and die a better man."

The Bible is your one sure guide to life. With the Bible to guide you, you never have to be lost.

OCTOBER 27

THE ARK OF SALVATION

By faith Noah . . . became one of those who are
made right with God through faith.
HEBREWS 11:7 ICB

Weather apps, sirens, and TV and radio stations keep us informed about the weather. We can be prepared for thunderstorms, tornadoes, and floods like we never could in the past because we get warnings in advance.

When God told Noah to build the ark because He was going to flood the earth, Noah believed God and obeyed Him. No one besides Noah's family believed the warning. People laughed at Noah and mocked his words and went about their daily lives without ever dreaming he might be right. God was speaking, but they ignored Him. Eventually only Noah and his family were saved from the flood.

You cannot come to Jesus unless the Spirit of God brings you. But what if you ignore His warnings? Eventually God will no longer be speaking to you, and then it will be too late. Come to Jesus while there is still time. Jesus is God's "greater Ark," ready to welcome you to safety today.

Are you in the Ark?

GOD IS NEVER LATE

The Lord is your keeper; the Lord is your shade at your right hand.

PSALM 121:5

In order for a tree to grow and bear fruit, its seed must first be planted in the ground and "die"—it gives up being a seed in order to become a plant.

In order for us to produce the fruit of the Spirit in our lives, we must first be planted in the Word of God and be willing to give up our selfish desires. As we obey God's Word, it nourishes our lives, and fruit begins to appear. You might show more patience with a younger sibling, or be kinder to the elderly couple next door.

But this doesn't happen overnight. It takes time and patience.

Joseph never would have been useful to God if he hadn't been sold by his brothers and then wrongly accused by Potiphar, who put him in prison. Even after he asked Pharaoh's cupbearer to tell Pharaoh of his unjust imprisonment, Joseph had to wait two more years to get out of prison. Then he became a ruler in Egypt at just the right time—when the nation needed help preparing for a great famine.

God might sometimes seem slow in coming to help us, but He never comes too late. His timing is always perfect.

CITIZENS OF HEAVEN

"Because I live, you will live also."
JOHN 14:19

People spend billions of dollars every year on skin creams, fitness machines, and all kinds of products claiming to make them live longer or slow down the aging process. But even the most beautiful or most physically fit people in the world will eventually grow old!

A day is coming, however, when everyone who knows Jesus will have perfect bodies—bodies that will never age or experience pain. Someday our dead bodies will be "raised in glory" (1 Corinthians 15:43)—and they will be transformed to be like Jesus' body after the resurrection.

Can I imagine what that will be like? No, not exactly. But I do know this: Jesus' body after the resurrection is the pattern or design for the new bodies we will have in Heaven. "For our citizenship is in heaven, from which we also eagerly wait for the Savior, the Lord Jesus Christ, who will transform our lowly body that it may be conformed to His glorious body" (Philippians 3:20–21).

And those new bodies will never grow old and will never die!

FINDING FULFILLMENT

"Let your soul delight itself in abundance."
ISAIAH 55:2

Counterfeit money isn't real money—it's an imitation. It might look like real money to most of us, but it has no value. It's a worthless substitute for the real thing.

Substitutes are what Satan tempted Jesus with in the desert at the beginning of His ministry, and he uses the same temptations today.

One trap was the lure of things. Jesus had fasted for forty days, and Satan tried to take advantage of His hunger by urging Him to use His supernatural power to turn stones into bread. But Jesus replied, "Man shall not live by bread alone, but by every word that proceeds from the mouth of God" (Matthew 4:4).

Food is important—but it isn't all-important. It's not a substitute for God's Word. Fun and recreation have their place in our lives—but not God's place. Money is necessary, but money must serve us; we should never worship money.

Isaiah said, "Let your soul delight itself in abundance." Yes, enjoy all that God gives you, both material and spiritual. Especially delight in the abundance of joy that comes from His presence.

Satan will always offer you substitutes. Tell him no!

THE HIGHEST CALLING

"Whoever of you does not forsake all that he has cannot be My disciple."
LUKE 14:33

An oil company once offered a missionary $10,000 to be its representative in the Far East. He turned down the offer. They raised their offer to $25,000, and he turned it down again. They raised it to $50,000, and he rejected the offer once more.

"What's wrong?" they asked.

"Your price is all right," he replied, "but your job is too small." God had called him to be a missionary. Nothing else was as important to him as that.

What should you be for Jesus—today, and when you grow up? Most Christians aren't called to be missionaries or preachers, but we all are called to follow Jesus. God tells us to be faithful wherever He puts us— at school, in the home, in the factory or office, in the neighborhood and nation. We all are called to be controlled by the Spirit and to bear the fruit of the Spirit. We are all called to be *ambassadors* for Jesus wherever God puts us—to represent and show Jesus to the people around us.

No job is as important as following Jesus!

NOVEMBER

The LORD is near to all who call upon Him,
to all who call upon Him in truth.
PSALM 145:18

PRAYER PARTNERS WITH GOD

The Spirit Himself makes intercession for us.
ROMANS 8:26

Sometimes we aren't sure how we should pray about a problem. Maybe it's because our situation is confusing. Other times our emotions are so strong—sadness or concern or fear—that we can't put them into words.

What a comfort these words should be: "The Spirit helps us in our weakness. We do not know what we ought to pray for, but the Spirit himself intercedes for us . . . in accordance with God's will" (Romans 8:26–27 NIV).

Think of it: even when we don't know how to pray, the Spirit knows our needs, and He brings our hearts before God's throne. That's what *intercession* is. The Spirit speaks to God for us! God isn't upset with us when we feel confused or overwhelmed. He simply cares and is there to help us. Although we can't understand how it happens, God the Holy Spirit prays for us to God the Father.

Turn to God in every situation—even when you don't feel like it. The Spirit is interceding for you perfectly.

TRUE HAPPINESS

Happy is he who has the God of Jacob for his help.

PSALM 146:5

How does a robin find worms to eat? First, it looks for visual cues of where a worm might be, near the surface of the ground. Then it flies to a spot where a worm seems to be, cocks its head, listens, and pecks where it hears the worm under the grass. Before long the robin flies off with its next meal. Its pursuit of the worm was a success.

In the Declaration of Independence, Thomas Jefferson wrote about "the pursuit of happiness." He was right to say that God has given us the freedom to pursue happiness. The problem is that so many people think this hunt for happiness must be the purpose of life. They spend their lives pursuing the things they think will make them happy.

True and lasting happiness can't happen unless you are pursuing God. He has promised, "You will seek Me and find Me, when you search for Me with all your heart" (Jeremiah 29:13). True and lasting happiness is called *joy*.

FAMILIES OF FAITH

Through wisdom a house is built, and by understanding it is established.
PROVERBS 24:3

If you walk through the preschool section at a toy store on your way to the video games, you'll see lots of toys related to family life: play kitchens and workbenches, dolls and strollers, construction vehicles and doctor kits. Someone has said that play is the young child's work, and that is true. In their families, children learn about life.

The family is the most important institution in the world. It was God's idea in the first place. Families existed before cities and governments, before written languages, nations, temples, and churches. In the home, children develop character, values, and goals. And in the home, children learn about God.

Today, Satan is attacking the family as never before. But as always, our best defense is the Word of God. What can you do to help your family be strong in the Lord? Read the Bible together as a family, have family devotions, and pray for one another daily by name.

If your family works together and pursues God together, imagine how strong you will be!

THE UNCERTAINTY OF LIFE

Teach us to number our days, that we may gain a heart of wisdom.

PSALM 90:12

What are your favorite activities? Do you enjoy art, music, sports, or reading? Who are the people you love? Who are your friends? One of the best things you can learn about life is that everything good in life is a gift from our loving God!

None of us can control the length of our lives. The Bible says people who understand this and learn to appreciate each day as a gift from God become wise. No matter how long we live, our time on earth—compared to eternity—is actually short. That's why God tells us to value the days we are given.

All of us will experience trouble and problems in our lives. In the Bible we read, "The length of our days is seventy years—or eighty, if we have the strength; yet their span is but trouble and sorrow, for they quickly pass, and we fly away" (Psalm 90:10 NIV).

But the Bible also gives us hope. It tells us that Jesus can help us each day of our lives, and that He has prepared a perfect place for us in Heaven.

Even your next breath is a gift from God. Live each day with thankfulness and "gain a heart of wisdom."

SATISFYING THE SOUL

Direct me in the path of your commands, for there I find delight.
PSALM 119:35 NIV

After a long bike ride, time on the ski slope, or practice with your team, you're hungry! Your body needs more food to use for fuel. And you're tired! Your muscles need time—plus good food and water—to rest and repair. If you want to do your best at sports, you need to take care of your body.

But did you know that you are more than just a body? Each of us is actually a living soul. Our souls are created in the image of God. God Himself has put His own nature within us!

Just as our bodies have characteristics and needs, so do our souls. The characteristics of the soul include intelligence, emotion, and will. The human soul longs for peace, contentment, and happiness. Most of all, the soul has an appetite and a need for God—a yearning to be connected to its Creator forever.

In our world, we are tempted to give most of our attention to taking care of our bodies and almost none to our souls. As a result, we can have healthy bodies but weak souls. The soul actually needs as much attention as the body.

How can you care for your soul today?

THE WEAPONS OF FAITH

This is the victory that overcomes the world, our faith.

1 JOHN 5:4 RSV

What would you do if you met a lion? You'd probably run, and you'd probably grab any weapon you could to fend him off if he attacked.

The Bible warns, "Stay alert! Watch out for your great enemy, the devil. He prowls around like a roaring lion, looking for someone to devour" (1 Peter 5:8 NLT).

One of Satan's tricks is to get our minds off the help God offers us every day. Satan tells us we have to fight our battles alone. But God knows we need His help.

When Satan tempts us to sin, our first response should be to run away. But if we are still attacked, we should use every weapon we have to win the fight against evil and temptation. The good news is this: God has provided the weapons! His Word, His angels, His Spirit, the encouragement and prayers of other believers—these and more are weapons God provides.

So when you are facing evil or temptation, tell a parent or other adult what is troubling you. Pray for God's help and direction. And remind yourself of Bible verses about how God helps you. You aren't in this battle alone—so pick up your faith weapons and fight!

WHAT IS JOY?

The joy of the LORD is your strength.
NEHEMIAH 8:10

D o you know someone who is just naturally happy and cheerful? Some people think Christians should always be smiling and happy, and something is wrong if they aren't. But this isn't necessarily true.

Jesus stood outside the tomb of His friend Lazarus, and we read that "Jesus wept" (John 11:35). As He approached Jerusalem, "He saw the city and wept" (Luke 19:41) because the people of God had rejected Him as their Savior. Before going to the cross, He knelt in the Garden of Gethsemane and was "in agony . . . [and] His sweat became like great drops of blood" (Luke 22:44).

Don't confuse happiness with joy. Happiness comes with happy situations; joy wells up deep inside our souls as we learn to trust Jesus no matter what happens. Having joy does not mean we are never sad or that we never cry. But joy is a quiet confidence, a peace that comes from God.

Problems can take away happiness, but they can never rob us of the joy God gives us. That joy is our strength for every day.

LIKE A SHEPHERD

He gathers the lambs in his arms and carries them close to his heart.

ISAIAH 40:11 NIV

The Old Testament gives a wonderful picture of God as our Shepherd. One psalm begins, "Hear us, O Shepherd of Israel, you who lead Joseph like a flock" (Psalm 80:1 NIV).

The almighty Creator of the universe cares for His people like a shepherd cares for his sheep! A shepherd protects and feeds his sheep and finds them when they stray. In the evening he brings them into the fold, safe from every enemy. Without the shepherd, the sheep would scatter and wander into danger.

In Psalm 23, the best-known of all psalms, David makes it personal: "The Lord is my shepherd. I have everything I need. . . . [His] goodness and love will be with me all my life" (vv. 1, 6 ICB). David knew God was constantly taking care of him every day until he went to Heaven.

But the New Testament tells of another Shepherd—the Lord Jesus Christ: "I am the good shepherd. The good shepherd gives His life for the sheep" (John 10:11). He guides and protects us, and even gave His life so we will be safely in His fold forever.

Will you look to Jesus to guide and protect you just like a shepherd guides and protects his flock?

AWAY WITH WORRY

The LORD is near to all who call upon Him, to all who call upon Him in truth.
PSALM 145:18

Are you a worrier? What are some things you *don't* worry about? Perhaps you never worry about whether you will be able to get water out of the faucet in your kitchen or whether a tree will fall on your house. Even the worst worrier in the world doesn't worry about some things!

Now ask yourself why you don't worry about those kinds of things. Is it because, in the case of running water, it has always been there when you wanted it? Or that a tree has never fallen on your house before? Being sure of something causes us to trust, doesn't it? (You may even live in a place where there are no tall trees.)

We can be just as certain and just as worry-free about God's love and protection. What is the evidence? It is the cross, where God fully expressed His love for us. The Bible says, "He who did not spare his own Son, but gave him up for us all—how will he not also, along with him, graciously give us all things?" (Romans 8:32 NIV).

God's love is certain. He has never gone back on a single promise, and He never will.

CREATED IN HIS IMAGE

If anyone is in Christ, he is a new creation.
2 CORINTHIANS 5:17

If your family's computer stops working, you don't take it to an auto mechanic for repairs. If the family car needs work, you don't take it to a plumber. If someone in your family needs an operation, you don't go to a computer repair store.

So doesn't it make sense that our spiritual problems—like selfishness, envy, and pride—can only be solved by the God who created us? He made us in His own image and likeness, and He knows all about us.

Today because of Jesus, we can be made new. And we can become like Him! First, when we put our faith in Jesus, we are born again by the Spirit of God. Then we can grow and become more like Jesus as the Spirit works in our lives. Selfishness, envy, pride, and other sins begin to fade into the past.

"Therefore, if anyone is in Christ, he is a new creation; old things have passed away; behold, all things have become new" (2 Corinthians 5:17). Look to Jesus, the only One who can repair hearts, to make you a new person in His image.

A HOME IN HEAVEN

You have a better possession and a lasting
one [prepared for you in heaven].
HEBREWS 10:34 AMP

Many people are never satisfied. They just want more and more. They act as though this life is all there is and whoever has the most possessions when they die "wins." How foolish!

First Corinthians 15:19 says, "If our hope in Christ is for this life only, we should be pitied more than anyone else in the world" (ICB). In other words, if there is no life after death, no Heaven, no promise of a better world—then we'll be extremely disappointed, and people should feel sorry for us. But this life is *not* all there is! Someday we'll be with our Father in Heaven, our true home, where all is happiness and peace. We will *not* be disappointed!

Knowing Heaven is real makes a difference in how we live. We won't become too attached to the things of this world. We will say with Paul, "I have learned in whatever state I am, to be content" (Philippians 4:11).

People will notice if you are content and wonder what is different about you. You can say that you are content with whatever you have in this world, because you are looking forward to Heaven! Tell them about Jesus and Heaven so they can learn to be content too.

A UNITED FAMILY

"All your children shall be taught by the LORD, and
great shall be the peace of your children."
ISAIAH 54:13

God created the family, and in His Word we find His instructions for how families should live. Those rules include putting others first instead of yourself and making people more important than things.

But family members don't always act in love. (If you have brothers and sisters, do you always get along, or do you sometimes fight?) From the time Adam and Eve sinned against God, the family has needed help.

What everyone does in your family makes a difference. You can help make your family a loving, close, and happy family if you ask God for His help and follow His ways. You can ask Him to help you be kind, to share, and to do your chores without complaining. You might even volunteer to do some extra chores when Mom and Dad are tired, like taking the dog for a walk or putting clean dishes away. And you can pray and ask God to help everyone in your family with whatever problems they face.

Practice these things with your parents and siblings today and every day. You'll be helping to make your home a happier, more peaceful place.

CLING AND HOPE

The LORD will be a shelter for His people.
JOEL 3:16

When storms like Hurricane Katrina cause flooding, it's not unusual for people to be rescued after hours of clinging to the rooftops of their homes. What people do in those situations brings to mind one slogan for life I've heard: "Cling and hope."

But cling to what? If you are waiting to be rescued from a flood, you don't want to cling to something that is sinking. Unfortunately, in daily life people often cling to their possessions and false ideas that can't help them. However, many others do find safety from the storms of life by putting their faith in a living God!

Turning to God during difficult times is always the right thing to do. Countless Christians throughout history have found that faith in Jesus is more than enough for whatever stress the day brings. Like a rescue boat helping someone off their roof in a flood, God rescues us and takes us to safety.

True Christians do more than "cling and hope." They know that with Jesus they are secure forever. How about you? Is your hope in Him?

GOD IN HUMAN FORM

[Christ] has gone into heaven and is at the right hand of God.
1 PETER 3:22

Often when someone is charged with a crime, a judge and jury will hear the evidence and facts in the case. The prosecution tries to prove the accused person is guilty, and the defense tries to prove the accused is innocent of the crime. The decision is based on the proof.

What proof does Jesus offer that He came to earth as God in human form?

First, there is the proof of His perfect life. He could ask, "Which of you convicts Me of sin?" (John 8:46)—and no one could answer.

Second, there is the evidence of His miracles. He showed that He had the power of God Almighty.

Third, the evidence of the prophecies He fulfilled. Hundreds of years before Jesus' birth, the prophets of the Old Testament spoke in detail about His death and resurrection.

Fourth, the evidence of His resurrection from the dead.

Fifth, the proof of changed lives. Jesus, the Son of God, has power to change the human heart. And He does.

Faith in Jesus is not a leap in the dark. It is based on the solid facts of Jesus' life, death, and resurrection. Thank God we have a solid foundation in Him!

"EVEN SO, COME!"

"Behold, I am coming quickly!"
REVELATION 22:7

What would you say about a person who had made a hundred promises to you and had already kept ninety-nine of them? You probably would think he was honest enough to fulfill the last promise, too, wouldn't you?

Jesus has fulfilled every promise He ever made, except one—He has not yet returned. Do you think He will?

Both the Old and New Testaments tell us about Jesus' return. For example, in the Old Testament, the prophet Isaiah looked forward to the day when the Messiah's kingdom would be a reality: "Behold, I create new heavens and a new earth; and the former shall not be remembered or come to mind" (Isaiah 65:17).

In the New Testament, in the gospel of John, Jesus says, "I go to prepare a place for you. And . . . I will come again and receive you to Myself" (14:2–3). The entire book of Revelation tells about the return of Christ. And we can say with the apostle John, who wrote that book, "Amen. Even so, come, Lord Jesus!" (22:20).

God's timing is perfect. Keep looking forward to Jesus' return, and seek to be His faithful follower until the day He comes to take those who love Him to Heaven.

DEALING WITH ETERNITY

I will see Your face in righteousness; I shall be
satisfied when I awake in your likeness.

PSALM 17:15

When English patriot Sir William Russell was about to die, he took his watch out of his pocket and handed it to the physician. "Would you kindly take my timepiece?" he asked. "I have no use for it. I am now dealing with eternity."

When we think of spending eternity in Heaven, we realize what is and is not important in our lives on earth. We should live every day with our eyes on eternity! Our faith in God and our hope for eternal life in Heaven with Him should affect what we do every day.

When the apostle Peter wrote about the future and Jesus' return, he said, "What manner of persons ought you to be in holy conduct and godliness? . . . Be diligent to be found by Him in peace, without spot and blameless" (2 Peter 3:11, 14). So when you are tempted to tell a lie, or be unkind to your sister, friend, or teammate, remember that you are a citizen of Heaven, and ask God to help you do the right thing.

How different would you act today if you knew tomorrow you would meet God face-to-face in Heaven? Today, be kind and faithful!

WE WILL SEE GOD

Our days on earth are as a shadow.
1 CHRONICLES 29:15

While playing a game or working on a crossword puzzle, have you ever said, "Give me a hint"? You wanted a clue to help you think of the answer you needed.

C. S. Lewis once said that life is only "shadowlands" compared with the glory to come. He meant that even life at its best is only a shadow, a hint, of what Heaven will be like. Sometimes the good things God gives us are hints of what is to come.

For example, we enjoy the beauty of God's creation. The colors, sights, and sounds of a fresh spring day, or beautiful flowers, or the glistening surf pounding a sandy beach—these give us a taste of an even greater beauty—the glory of Heaven.

Take delight in the good things God gives you. The Bible reminds us, "Every good gift and every perfect gift is from above, and comes down from the Father of lights" (James 1:17). And every one of His good gifts should remind us that one day we will see God face-to-face and live with Him forever!

NO SUBSTITUTES

I will both lie down in peace, and sleep; for You
alone, O LORD, make me dwell in safety.

PSALM 4:8

Using drugs or alcohol to escape our problems or cope with them never works.

I'm not a doctor, of course, and I fully realize medications can be useful with a doctor's help. But in my experience far too many people turn first to drugs or alcohol instead of to God. Rather than face their problems and deal with them with God's help, they just end up creating more problems. Such "solutions" never work and only make things worse. No wonder the book of Proverbs warns that alcohol "at the last . . . bites like a serpent, and stings like a viper" (Proverbs 23:32).

Don't let anyone convince you that using drugs or alcohol is a good way to deal with your problems. And don't let anything substitute for God. He loves you, and He wants to give you peace—the peace that comes from knowing Him and His love and care for you. He wants you to sleep peacefully at night. Jesus' promise to His followers is true: "I will give you rest" (Matthew 11:28).

SUNSHINE AND SHADOW

If you should suffer for righteousness' sake, you are blessed.
1 PETER 3:14

All the masterpieces of painting contain both light and shadow. An artist uses both light and dark paint to show certain features of his subject, and together they reveal beauty or character.

A happy life isn't filled only with sunshine. It has both light and shadow—good times and bad times—to bring beauty. Troubles can become blessings because they can form a dark backdrop for the radiance of the Christian life.

It's always been true that the greatest musicians could bring songs out of sadness. Fanny Crosby was blind, but she had a bright spirit because of her strong faith in Jesus. She "saw" more than most of us do with normal vision and gave us great gospel songs that cheer our hearts and lives.

Paul and Silas sang a song of praise at midnight in a rat-infested jail in Philippi. Their patience in a hard situation led to the prison warden and his family becoming Christians.

Don't be discouraged by the hard things, the "shadows" God brings into your life. He can use them to make a masterpiece!

ABIDING PEACE

"Fear not, for I am with you; be not dismayed, for I am your God."

ISAIAH 41:10

Whenever I think of God's faithfulness in the midst of suffering, I think of my friend Corrie ten Boom, the remarkable Dutch woman who, with her family, hid Jews from the Nazis during World War II. After being imprisoned in a concentration camp at Ravensbruck, Germany, Corrie spent her life traveling the world to tell her story of suffering, forgiveness, and joy.

For thirty-five years she never had a permanent home, but when she was eighty-five and in poor health, some friends gave her a lovely house in California. It was a luxury she never dreamed she would have and never would have gone after on her own.

One day a friend was visiting. He said, "Corrie, hasn't God been good to give you this beautiful house?"

She replied firmly, "Jimmy, God was good when I was in Ravensbruck too!" In the torture of a prison camp, and when she was in a beautiful home, Corrie believed all the time that God is good.

Most of us will never experience the horrors Corrie knew. But no matter what we face, we can depend on God's promise: "Fear not; for I am with you." We serve a good God. All the time, God is good.

THANKFUL IN PRAYER

Devote yourselves to prayer, being watchful and thankful.
COLOSSIANS 4:2 NIV

Prayer isn't just asking God for something we want. When we pray, we should also confess our sins and praise God for who He is and what He has done for us.

We want to be thankful to God when we pray too. Over and over the Bible tells us to give thanks and gives us examples of thankful people. The psalmist said, "Oh, give thanks to the LORD, for He is good! For His mercy endures forever" (Psalm 107:1). When Jesus turned the little boy's lunch into a meal for five thousand people, He waited until after "he had given thanks" (Matthew 15:36 NIV) to share the food. And at the Last Supper with His disciples, before He faced the cross, Jesus "gave thanks" (Luke 22:17, 19).

It's easy to be thankful when God blesses us with something good—recovery from a sickness, for example, or a family who loves us. But the Bible says we should "give thanks in all circumstances, for this is God's will for [us] in Christ Jesus" (1 Thessalonians 5:18 NIV).

Make thankfulness part of your prayers every day.

THE GRACE OF GRATITUDE

It is good to give thanks to the Lord.

PSALM 92:1

On Thanksgiving Day you will probably eat a wonderful feast, but the Pilgrims who landed at Plymouth in 1620 could not have imagined the prosperity we enjoy today. During that first long winter, many graves had to be dug. Seeds from England failed to grow crops, and a ship that was supposed to bring food and supplies brought thirty-five more mouths to feed—and not an ounce of food or provisions.

Yet the Pilgrims constantly gave thanks for all they had. They caught fish and hunted wild fowl and venison. They had some Indian corn. On one occasion a Pilgrim leader finished a plain dinner of clams and water and gave thanks to God "for the abundance of the sea and the treasures hid in the sand."

According to today's standards, these people had little, but they had a sense of great gratitude. Gratitude is one of the greatest Christian virtues; ingratitude is one of the most destructive sins. Ask God to open your eyes to all the blessings He has given you, and ask for a fresh spirit of gratitude—not just at this season of the year, but always.

GOD'S HOLINESS

Holy, holy, holy is the LORD of hosts; the whole earth is full of His glory!
ISAIAH 6:3

From Genesis to Revelation, God reveals Himself as holy and pure—very different from sinful human beings. He is so holy that our sin separates us from Him.

Jesus cried from the cross, "My God, My God, why have You forsaken Me?" (Mark 15:34). Jesus never sinned, but on the cross the sin of all people was laid upon Him. What a horrible moment! Jesus endured the ultimate punishment for our sins—the punishment of being separated from the presence of His Father. Jesus did not deserve any punishment, but He took the punishment we deserved for our sins.

If you were asked to name the things you are thankful for, what would you include? Perhaps your family, health, friends, church—and those wouldn't be wrong. We should be grateful for every gift God gives us. But the greatest gift of all is the gift of His Son, who endured the penalty we deserved for our sin so we could be brought back to our holy God again.

Never take that gift for granted! "Thanks be to God for His indescribable gift!" (2 Corinthians 9:15).

TRUE THANKSGIVING

Oh, give thanks to the LORD, for He is good!

PSALM 107:1

Separated from friends, unjustly accused, brutally treated—if any man had a right to complain, it was this man sitting almost forgotten in a harsh Roman prison. But instead of complaints, he had words of praise and thanksgiving!

This was the apostle Paul—a man who had learned the meaning of true thanksgiving, even in the midst of great hardship. Look carefully at what he wrote during that prison experience: "Sing and make music in your heart to the Lord, always giving thanks to God the Father for everything, in the name of our Lord Jesus Christ" (Ephesians 5:19–20 NIV).

Think of it! "Always giving thanks . . . for everything," no matter the situation. His guards and fellow prisoners must have thought he was crazy—but that didn't stop him. Paul knew that even when things are bad, God is always good.

For Paul, thanksgiving was not a once-a-year celebration, but a daily reality that made him a joyful person in every situation. Make a list of all the wonderful things you have to be thankful for today!

NOVEMBER 25

GOD'S LOVE

This is how God showed his love among us: He
sent his one and only Son into the world.

1 JOHN 4:9 NIV

Human beings of all ages need love. Without love, babies can fail to grow. Kids need love. Parents need love. Older people need love. Love has been the subject of thousands of books, songs, and movies. On Valentine's Day we celebrate love. One of the most familiar verses in the Bible is John 3:16, just twenty-five beautiful words: "For God so loved the world that He gave His only begotten Son, that whoever believes in Him should not perish but have everlasting life."

But many people don't understand God's love. "God is love" does not mean that everything is sweet, beautiful, and happy. It doesn't mean that God is fine with whatever happens or that He couldn't possibly allow punishment for sin.

Here's what "God is love" means: because God is holy, all sin must be punished, but because God is love, He sent His Son from Heaven to give His life as the final and perfect sacrifice for sin.

But we must respond. We must believe. We must commit our lives to Jesus and trust Him as our Savior and Lord. Have you decided to put your faith in Him and accept the amazing love God has for you?

WISDOM FROM ABOVE

The wisdom that is from above is first pure, then peaceable.

JAMES 3:17

Today there is more knowledge in the world than ever before, and information can be sent in a millisecond to nearly any part of the globe. More facts have been discovered in the past one hundred years than in all other centuries combined! But facts and information are not the same as wisdom. We can be full of facts and knowledge and not be wise.

The Bible says there are two kinds of wisdom in the world. First, there is wisdom that is given by God: "The wisdom from above is first of all pure. It is also peace loving, gentle at all times, and willing to yield to others. It is full of mercy and the fruit of good deeds. It shows no favoritism and is always sincere" (James 3:17 NLT). People with godly wisdom know how to use information to make choices that please God.

The second kind of wisdom is the "wisdom of this world" (1 Corinthians 3:19). This wisdom leaves God and His commands out of human decisions and tries to solve problems without Him. But this never works for long.

Which kind of wisdom will you choose?

TRAVELING TO HEAVEN

The Lord will . . . preserve me for His heavenly kingdom.
2 TIMOTHY 4:18

Preparing for Heaven can be compared to getting ready for a vacation. First, you must decide you want to go there. Next, you must purchase your ticket.

But wait! How will you purchase it? Can you buy it by being a good person? Or going to church or Sunday school? Or giving money or volunteering your time to help others? The Bible says none of these will get you a ticket, because the ticket to Heaven is far too expensive for any human being to afford.

Does that mean we can never go there? No—and the reason is because Someone else has already purchased the ticket for us! That Person was Jesus, and the price He paid was His own blood, shed on the cross for us.

Now He offers us the ticket to Heaven, free and fully paid! Why would you ever want to refuse it? Why try some other way? Jesus' invitation is still open: "'Come!' Whoever is thirsty, let him come; and whoever wishes, let him take the free gift of the water of life" (Revelation 22:17 NIV).

GIVING TO GOD

Honor the LORD with your possessions.
PROVERBS 3:9

God doesn't *need* our money to get His work done. Everything is God's, and He can do anything without our help. But it is part of His plan that His people live and give generously.

At least two things happen when we give. First, when we give with the right attitude, God reminds us that what we have isn't really ours. He gave us everything we have, and it actually all belongs to Him! King David prayed, "All things come from You, and of Your own we have given You" (1 Chronicles 29:14). This is an important truth to learn.

Second, when we give, we help meet the needs of other people God also loves. By giving to others, we show them God's love, and we point them to the greatest Gift of all—God's gift of His Son for our salvation.

Our lives should be like a river, not a lake. A lake stores water; a river sends it out. God wants us to be a river of blessing to others. How could you send out God's love to others this week?

A HEAVENLY ADDRESS

"I am going there to prepare a place for you."
JOHN 14:2 NIV

What city do you live in? Have you ever moved to a new home or apartment and had to learn a new address? What is your current address?

I live in a place high on a mountain in a log cabin in North Carolina. I may travel all over the world, but I know that when I come home, I will return to that exact location. It will still be there at the end of my journey, and I always look forward to coming home!

When Jesus said He was going to Heaven to prepare a place for us, He was telling us that when we die, we are going to an exact location. We do not evaporate or disappear. In fact, Jesus said, "In My Father's house are many mansions" (John 14:2). We are going to have a place in Heaven if we have trusted Jesus as our Savior—and not just any place, but a mansion!

When Christians die, we go straight into Jesus' presence—straight to that place He has prepared, straight to that mansion in Heaven to spend eternity with God. We are simply changing our address!

GOD'S TRUTH

You are my hiding place. . . . I hope in Your word.
PSALM 119:114

Day changes to night. Seasons change—winter, spring, summer, fall. The calendar changes from month to month. Parents change jobs, and children change schools. But God's Word never changes.

Jesus said, "I tell you the truth, until heaven and earth disappear, not the smallest letter, not the least stroke of a pen, will by any means disappear from the Law" (Matthew 5:18 NIV). He also said, "Heaven and earth will pass away, but My words will by no means pass away" (Matthew 24:35).

God knows what is best for us. He knows everything about us, and He knows the problems we face. If He didn't love us, He wouldn't guide us in the right path. But He does! If He didn't love us, He wouldn't have made a way for us to know Him. But He did!

Only God's Word can help us avoid the wrong way and lead us in the right way. Psalm 119 says, "Your word is a lamp to my feet and a light to my path" (v. 105). Only God's Word shows us who He is and gives us hope for the future.

Let God's Word shape and guide you and give you hope today!

DECEMBER

How great is the love the Father has lavished on
us, that we should be called children of God!

1 JOHN 3:1 NIV

DECEMBER 1

UNENDING GRACE

Grace and truth came through Jesus Christ.
JOHN 1:17

When you think of grace, you might first think about a bird soaring in the sky or a cheetah running through the jungle or a swan floating on water. Whatever you picture, grace always makes us think of something or someone beautiful.

But the most beautiful thought about grace is God's grace. It means He's kind to us, gentle with us, and giving us His mercy and undeserved favor. It means God owes us nothing, and we deserve nothing from Him. When the Bible says, "By grace you have been saved" (Ephesians 2:5), it means we did nothing, and could do nothing, to earn salvation. God saved us because of His grace.

God's love is the reason He gives us His grace, but how does He do it? Through Jesus' death on the cross. Jesus paid the price for our sin even though we did not deserve it. That is grace—the love of God for a sinful world.

God also shows His grace when we humbly bow before Jesus in repentance and faith, for then we find forgiveness. Thank God for His grace! For it is God's Riches at Christ's Expense.

SIN'S DEADLY HERITAGE

The creation itself will be liberated from its bondage to decay.
ROMANS 8:21 NIV

Once some computers in our office were attacked by a computer virus. The staff suddenly found their computers unable to function as they were designed to do. Only a major reprogramming restored the hard drives and made the computers useful again.

I couldn't help but compare this to another virus—the "virus" of sin. God created Adam and Eve perfect and without sin. They had a close relationship with God, and He provided for everything they needed. But then they turned against God and sin entered the world, and since that day the human heart has been infected with the deadly virus of sin. This virus destroyed our close relationship with God, and even all creation was affected.

But Jesus came to conquer the virus of sin! When He comes into our lives, He begins to remake us from within. As we read God's Word and listen to Jesus, our hearts are reprogrammed. The virus no longer has control.

Someday God will remove the virus of sin forever, and all creation will be set free and made new. Until then, let Jesus reprogram your life today and every day.

DECEMBER 3

FROM TIME TO ETERNITY

We give thanks to . . . God . . . because of the
hope which is laid up for you in heaven.
COLOSSIANS 1:3, 5

Once when I was in London, England, I stood in a crowd to watch Queen Elizabeth return home from an overseas trip. There was quite a parade—with high-ranking officials, marching bands, military troops, and waving flags. I saw all the splendor that is part of a queen's homecoming.

But that was nothing compared to the homecoming of a true believer!

From our human viewpoint, someone's death is always a sad time. And of course it isn't wrong to be sad about the loss of a loved one. Jesus wept at the grave of His friend Lazarus (John 11:35). But for Christians death is not a tragedy. Believers who die enter Heaven itself! They're carried up by the angels to a glorious welcome (Luke 16:22).

The apostle Paul said we should not "grieve like the rest of men, who have no hope" (1 Thessalonians 4:13 NIV). Yes, we have hope! The way to Heaven may involve walking through the valley of the shadow of death, but the angels are with us all the way—and beyond is Heaven, our glorious home.

BE STRONG

Walk in Him, rooted and built up in Him.
COLOSSIANS 2:6–7

Not far from our home in North Carolina is Mount Mitchell, the highest point in the eastern United States. The mountains in that area are filled with old trees that have been stunted and gnarled by the hostile climate and rocky soil.

But local craftsmen have told me that when one of these trees finally dies, its wood is highly prized—and the reason is that it is so strong. The tree resisted those fierce alpine winds for many years, and all that effort made it strong.

What happens when you face problems, when the winds of trouble blow in your life? Do they flatten you, knock you down, and stop your growth? Or, like those trees, do you grow stronger?

What makes the difference? The trees that survive, I am told, are those with the deepest roots. The roots are like an anchor helping them survive the winds and storms, and they also draw up the soil's nutrients, helping the trees grow stronger.

Be like one of those trees. Make sure you are firmly planted in Jesus and His Word, so you may be "rooted and built up in Him and established in the faith" (Colossians 2:7).

DECEMBER 5

TWICE BORN

"Unless one is born again, he cannot see the kingdom of God."
JOHN 3:3

Have you ever seen a newborn baby or held a new brother or sister carefully on your lap? Even rough-and-tough dads and big brothers feel amazed by the sweetness of a baby—soft cheeks, big eyes, and small hands that wrap tightly around our fingers.

We can't fully explain the mystery of a new life, but we accept its wonder. So why do people sometimes have trouble accepting the reality and wonder of *spiritual* rebirth—of being "born again"? To those who have experienced it or seen it happen in others, it is just as real as physical birth.

God causes the acorn to produce the mighty oak tree. He created the universe out of nothing. He puts life into the cells that will form a tiny infant. And He places His divine life in the hearts of those who earnestly seek Him through Jesus.

This is not guessing; it is fact. Has it happened to you? If not, by a simple prayer of faith, ask Jesus into your life right now. He will come in, and you will be born again!

THE JOY OF CHRISTMAS

When they saw the star, they rejoiced with exceedingly great joy.

MATTHEW 2:10

Are you looking forward to Christmas? Do you get excited thinking about that day? Sometimes it feels like Christmas Day will never arrive.

I wonder if the wise men were excited as they followed the star. As they traveled hundreds of miles across the desert, did they feel that the time would never come when they would see the newborn king? It took them months to prepare for the trip and make the journey. They had put a lot of effort into getting special, expensive gifts for the child. I'm sure that they couldn't wait to worship Jesus! In fact, the Bible says that as the star led them to Bethlehem near the end of their journey, they felt "exceedingly great joy."

The Christmas season can get busy with shopping, wish lists, and parties. Sometimes it's hard to remember the reason for all the celebration. Remember the wise men. Their focus was totally on Jesus, the One who would be called "Immanuel, . . . God with us" (Matthew 1:23). So focus on Jesus this Christmas. Take time every day to read the Bible about His coming and the wonderful story of His birth. You will make this Christmas one of "exceedingly great joy"!

DECEMBER 7

GOD SEES ALL

Great is our Lord and mighty in power; his understanding has no limit.
PSALM 147:5 NIV

Some years ago a friend of mine was standing on top of a mountain in North Carolina. The roads were filled with curves, and it was difficult to see very far ahead. This man saw two cars heading toward each other. He realized they couldn't see each other. Then a third car pulled up alongside one of the others and began to pass it—and the passing car was headed straight into the path of the car coming from the other direction. My friend shouted a warning, but the drivers couldn't hear, and there was a terrible crash.

This is how our all-knowing God looks on us. He sees what has happened, what is happening, and what will happen. He also sees us when we foolishly think we can get by with breaking His laws, or we act out of sinful pride or lust or anger. Like the man on that mountain, He shouts His warnings at us—but we are too busy or too stubborn to listen.

God sees the whole picture. He knows what is best for us, and He knows what will harm us. Don't think your way is better than His, but listen to His Word—and obey.

LEARNING FROM OUR PARENTS

Train up a child in the way he should go, and when
he is old he will not depart from it.
PROVERBS 22:6

Parents want their children to know right from wrong, and the best place to learn it is at home. That's why good parents set rules and discipline their children. You might be upset sometimes by a rule or a consequence you experience. But you would be upset if you were never taught or disciplined! The Bible says, "He who loves him disciplines him promptly" (Proverbs 13:24).

The Bible also encourages parents and children to talk about God and His ways as they go about their daily lives together: "These words which I command you today shall be in your heart. You shall teach them diligently to your children, and shall talk of them when you sit in your house, when you walk by the way, when you lie down, and when you rise up" (Deuteronomy 6:6–7).

Be thankful for your parents and all they teach you. Especially be thankful for everything they teach you about God, His love, and living your life every day for Him!

DECEMBER 9

NOT INTERESTED

Behold, God is great, and we do not know Him.
JOB 36:26

One evening in Jerusalem I looked out my hotel window and saw the lights of Bethlehem in the distance. I thought about the response of the innkeeper when Mary and Joseph wanted to find a room where Mary's baby could be born. The Bethlehem innkeeper probably wanted to help them. But his inn was crowded, his hands were full, and his mind was preoccupied.

Perhaps he told Mary and Joseph, "I wish I could help you, but I must keep my priorities. After all, this is a business, and this coming child is no real concern of mine. But I'm not a hard-hearted man. Over there is the stable. You are welcome to use it if you care to. That is the best I can do. Now I must get back to my work. My guests need me."

Many people who hear the gospel give that same answer today. You might have friends who just aren't concerned about spiritual things. They are simply too interested in other things to welcome Jesus into their lives. Don't let that happen to you—and keep praying for those friends to want to know God too.

OUR JOURNEY TO GOD

He is able to keep what I have committed to Him until that Day.

2 TIMOTHY 1:12

Many times I have said good-bye to my wife and children as I left home to preach in a place far away. Departures and good-byes always have a twinge of sadness, but there is also the happy expectation that we will be together again.

Everything that happens in our lives is like the preparation before a big journey. Just as campers will map out their route and load up food and supplies before they leave, we should spend our time on this earth preparing for our journey into eternity.

The Bible speaks of death as a *departure*, which in Paul's time literally meant to pull up anchor and set sail. When Paul approached the valley of the shadow of death, he did not shudder with fear. Instead, he announced with a note of triumph, "The time of my departure is at hand" (2 Timothy 4:6).

That's the sure hope of every believing Christian whose loved one has departed to be with the Lord. We say good-bye, but only until Jesus returns and we are together with the Lord forever.

DECEMBER 11

GOD SENT HIS SON

For in Christ lives all the fullness of God in a human body.
COLOSSIANS 2:9 NLT

On that first Christmas night in Bethlehem, "God was manifested in the flesh" (1 Timothy 3:16). *Manifested* means "shown" or "revealed." God revealed Himself to us in the person of Jesus.

What an incredible truth! Think of it: the God of the universe took human form! In the words of "Hark! The Herald Angels Sing," the familiar Christmas carol, "Veiled in flesh the Godhead see; hail the incarnate Deity."

If you want to know what God is like, then take a long look at Jesus—because He was God in human flesh. He showed us God's wisdom, power, and majesty, and His justice, mercy, grace, and love. "The Word was God. . . . And the Word became flesh and dwelt among us" (John 1:1, 14).

To His disciples Jesus said, "You believe in God, believe also in Me" (John 14:1). If we believe in what God made and what God said, we will also believe in the One God sent. And if we have any doubts about what God is like, we only have to look at Jesus.

HIS NAME IS WONDERFUL

God also has . . . given Him the name which is above every name.

PHILIPPIANS 2:9

Over two thousand years ago, on a night the world has come to call Christmas, a young Jewish woman went through the experience countless mothers had before her: she had a baby.

But this birth was like no other in history. For one thing, this Child had no human father. As the angel had promised Mary, "The Holy Spirit will come upon you, and the power of the Highest will overshadow you" (Luke 1:35). Mary had humbly replied, "Let it be to me according to your word" (Luke 1:38).

This also was like no other birth because of the Child who was born. Jesus was no ordinary Child. He was the unique Son of God, sent from Heaven to save us from our sins. "He humbled Himself and became obedient to the point of death, even the death of the cross. Therefore God also has highly exalted Him and given Him the name which is above every name" (Philippians 2:8–9).

The Christmas season is full of glitter and fun and can be a very busy time. But remember the miracle of that first Christmas. With the wise men, let us fall down and worship Him, the Son of God, the Savior Jesus (Matthew 2:11).

THE NIGHT OF LIGHT

"I am the light of the world. He who follows
Me shall not walk in darkness."
JOHN 8:12

This month the birthday of Jesus will be celebrated all over the world—in various ways, in many languages, by people of all races. People will exchange gifts and talk about Jesus, the Prince of Peace. Homes, churches, and businesses are decorated with glowing, colorful lights.

Imagine the scene in Bethlehem two thousand years ago. It began just like any other night. But it became the most significant night of history. It became the night of light! This was the night God brought into the world the One who is "the light of the world."

In nearby fields, shepherds saw great light as angels filled the sky and praised God for His gift of Jesus. Far away to the east, wise men saw a new star in the sky and understood that it meant a new King had been born.

Someday Jesus will return to earth and there will be no more night, because He is the Light. As you look at the lights of this Christmas season, think of Jesus, the Light of the World, and allow His light to shine in your life too!

OUR LOVING, COMPASSIONATE GOD

"I am the bread of life."
JOHN 6:35

Our bodies need food for fuel and nutrition. When Jesus said, "I am the bread of life," He was saying that while we need food for our physical bodies, we need Him even more. Jesus came to the world so we could know without a doubt that God cares about us and all our needs.

God's written Word, the Bible, tells us of His love. But Jesus is the *Living Word*. Everything about Jesus' life *demonstrates*, or shows, God's love for us in very clear ways.

Every time He fed the hungry, He was saying, "I am the bread of life." Every time He healed someone who was sick, He was saying, "I am the Great Physician." Every move Jesus made, every miracle He performed, every word He spoke demonstrated who He is and showed the truth and the love of God to a lost world.

The apostle Paul wrote, "God demonstrates His own love toward us, in that while we were still sinners, Christ died for us" (Romans 5:8). Yes, God made His great love very clear by sending His Son! Jesus, the Bread of Life, is everything we need.

THE NAMES OF OUR SAVIOR

You are the Christ, the Son of the living God.
MATTHEW 16:16

The Bible has many names, descriptions, and titles for Jesus. Some are easy to understand, like "Friend," "Teacher," and "Healer." Jesus was a Friend to children. He stopped His work to talk with them and bless them even when the disciples thought He was too busy. He taught people about God wherever He went. He made sick people well and blind people see.

Some of the Bible's names for Jesus make us think a little more—like "Christ," "Messiah," and "Son of God."

The title *Christ* means "anointed one." It is the Greek term for the Hebrew word *Messiah*. Both words mean the "anointed one" or "sent one"—the One chosen and sent by God to save His people.

Jesus is called "God's Son" because Jesus is God! He has always existed with God. Another reason for the name is that Jesus represented God on earth like a son represents his father. Jesus' words and actions and all His names show us what God "looks like." He is our Friend, Teacher, Healer, and Savior!

THE COST OF LOVE

How great is the love the Father has lavished on us,
that we should be called children of God!

1 JOHN 3:1 NIV

Mary and Joseph deeply loved the child God gave them. They even became refugees to spare Jesus' life when King Herod tried to kill Him (Matthew 2:13).

But God loved His Son even more. The Bible says, "The Father loves the Son, and has given all things into His hand" (John 3:35). Your parents miss you when you go away for a week of summer camp. Can you imagine the Father's emotions as His dearly loved Son left Heaven for earth? He knew that Jesus would one day go to the cross. He knew that Jesus would be "despised and rejected by men, a man of sorrows, and familiar with suffering" (Isaiah 53:3 NIV). We all like to think about how much God loves us. But let's remember what it cost the Father to send His beloved Son into the world.

Why did He do it? Because "God so loved the world that He gave His only begotten Son, that whoever believes in Him should not perish but have everlasting life" (John 3:16).

God loves the Son—and He loves you too!

JESUS FOR EVERYONE

Bless the LORD . . . who forgives all your iniquities,
who heals all your diseases.
PSALM 103:2–3

Jesus came into the world to save all kinds of people. One way God showed us this is true was by inviting two different groups of people to worship Jesus when He was born.

One group was the shepherds—poor, looked down on, uneducated. The other was the wise men—highly educated, rich, respected. The two groups could not have been more different!

God brought both groups to Bethlehem—one by the angel's announcement, one by the appearance of a miraculous star. And by bringing both, God was telling us that Jesus is the Savior for everyone. Every person needs His forgiveness and new life—and everyone can have it, if they repent and come to the Christ of Christmas.

No matter who you are in the eyes of others, you need Jesus. And no matter what you have or don't have, He loves you and stands ready to welcome you today.

PERFECT PEACE

"Your faith has saved you. Go in peace."
LUKE 7:50

During World War I, on Christmas Eve, the battlefield was strangely quiet. As soft snow fell, soldiers thought about their homes and families far away. Then one young man began to hum "Silent Night." Others joined in, filling the trenches with the Christmas song.

When they finished they were astonished to hear the song in another language, coming from the trenches across the battlefield. The other soldiers also sang "Silent Night"! That night both sides of the battle were thinking of the Prince of Peace, the Christ of Christmas.

Wouldn't it be wonderful if all the world could unite around Jesus, that "Holy Infant, so tender and mild"? Full peace will come only when Jesus returns. But until that day we can know His peace in our hearts, and we can be messengers of His peace in the world. Faith in Jesus is what brings peace.

A BETTER WORLD

The LORD is near to all who call upon Him, to all who call upon Him in truth.
PSALM 145:18

Have you ever thought about all that has happened to the world because Jesus came? The Baby in the manger of Bethlehem grew up to become our crucified and risen Savior—and the world has never been the same!

Because they obeyed Jesus' command "Whatever you wish that others would do to you, do also to them" (Matthew 7:12 ESV), Christians around the world have built hospitals, orphanages, relief agencies, and universities. They have fought for the abolition of slavery and education for all. In these activities and many more, followers of Jesus have let the world know about His love.

Jesus' compassion has made the world more compassionate. His healing touch has made the world kinder. His selflessness has made the world more humble. Christ drew a circle of hope around the shoulders of men and women and gave them something to live for.

If Jesus had not come, this world would be a lost world. Sinful people would have no access to God. There would be no forgiveness. But Jesus *did* come into the world, and He made it a better place. He will do the same for you, if you will open your life to Him.

THE KING OF KINGS

Your throne will last forever and ever. You will
rule your kingdom with fairness.

PSALM 45:6 ICB

"My kingdom is not of this world," Jesus said (John 18:36). For that reason, many people didn't recognize Jesus as a king. But He is! And not just a king, but the King of kings—the Ruler over all.

A king is the highest in the land. All other people are his subjects and do what the king wants them to do. Jesus taught that His followers need to be fully devoted to Him. His miracles and His resurrection proved He has power over all the earth and over life and death. There is no one higher. That is why He is the King of kings and Lord of lords.

Jesus' kingdom is real, even though it's not like the nations and kingdoms of the world. It is a kingdom where what is done is right and good. Those who have received Jesus Christ as Savior are part of His kingdom.

And someday, when God says the time is right, Jesus will return to earth. Then His kingdom will fill the whole earth! And like the apostle Thomas, when he recognized Jesus after His resurrection, we will bow down and say, "My Lord and my God!" (John 20:28).

GOD WITH US

Behold, the virgin shall conceive and bear a Son,
and shall call His name Immanuel.
ISAIAH 7:14

Christmas is a joyous time, but many people feel troubled at this time of year. Because they are lonely, the gladness of the Christmas season makes their loneliness feel even worse. Can you think of anyone at school or in your neighborhood who might feel this way?

Christmas is God's reminder that we are *not* alone. Jesus' life, death, and resurrection show us God's love, which rescues us from separation and loneliness. God came down from Heaven to tell us He loves us! The name *Immanuel* means "God with us."

At this Christmas season, you can be certain that Jesus is here. He is here to give us hope, to forgive our sins, to give us a new song, to give us faith, and to heal our hearts if we will let Him. Christians are people who have said yes to Jesus, and now we can share His love with others.

The Christmas message never changes. Christmas still reminds us that God is with us. If you are lonely this Christmas, welcome Jesus into your life. Then ask Him to help you reach out to someone else who needs to know the good news of Jesus' love.

TO THE RESCUE!

"I have come that they may have life, and that
they may have it more abundantly."
JOHN 10:10

Christmas is almost here! Have you wrapped the presents you are giving to others? Have you thought about how you will honor and worship Jesus on His birthday?

Christmas is not a day for selfishness and focusing on the things we receive. Christmas is about giving. We celebrate the gift that made Heaven sing—the birth of Jesus, sent to save us from our sins!

Christmas tells us that at a specific time and at a specific place, a specific person was born. In the words of a favorite carol "Silent Night," that person was the "Holy Infant, so tender and mild"—the Lord, Jesus Christ. He came "to seek and to save that which was lost" (Luke 19:10).

God has not left us alone. He gave us Jesus to rescue us! He wants us to experience life the way He created it to be. What a wonderful gift! So this Christmas, be sure you are truly ready to celebrate the very best Gift of all: Jesus.

DECEMBER 23

A HEALING WORD

"I have called you friends."
JOHN 15:15

Jesus came into a world that had the same kinds of problems our world has today—poverty, disease, injustice, and idol worship (making things more important than Jesus). And the words He spoke to people then He still speaks to people today.

People living with great sadness hear, "I have come that they may have life, and that they may have it more abundantly" (John 10:10).

People who feel the guilt of sin hear, "Be of good cheer; your sins are forgiven" (Matthew 9:2).

People without friends hear, "No longer do I call you servants . . . but I have called you friends" (John 15:15).

Jesus has healing words for everyone. Even though the world looks different now than it did when Jesus lived on earth, our problems are the same—for they are problems of the heart. And Jesus still comes to us today to cleanse our guilt, give us hope for the future, and heal our hurts with His love. What healing words does Jesus have for you today?

LOOKING FOR PEACE

Glory to God in the highest, and on earth peace.

LUKE 2:14

Tonight is Christmas Eve. It just might be the most peaceful night of the year. Most businesses and restaurants close. Families and friends gather for special suppers, attend church services together, and sing carols. Some open gifts. There's a wonderful sense of celebration and expectation in the air, because tomorrow is Christmas Day.

On the night Jesus was born, angels appeared to shepherds tending their sheep in the fields outside Bethlehem. Those angels announced the Savior's birth and promised peace on earth. The centuries have rolled by, and still the world longs for the peace the angels said would come because Jesus had been born. But much of the world experiences violence and conflict. "Where is His peace?" some may ask.

I know where it is. It's in the hearts of all who have trusted His grace.

We can have peace—peace with God, peace in our hearts, and peace with each other—as we give ourselves to Jesus as our Lord. Has this peace come into your life?

ROOM FOR JESUS

She brought forth her firstborn Son, . . . and laid Him in a
manger, because there was no room for them in the inn.
LUKE 2:7

Through the years, Christmas picture books have shown the animals in the stable where Jesus was born in Bethlehem. The animals always have room for Jesus in their stable, even though Bethlehem didn't have room for Jesus in the inn.

No room for Jesus? No room for the King of kings? That's how it was in Bethlehem when Jesus was born. The inn was full, and Mary and Joseph spent the night in a shelter meant for sheep and cows and donkeys. Jesus' bed was an animal's feeding trough, called a *manger*, filled with hay. There was no room for Jesus in the world He had made—imagine!

The first verse of a favorite Christmas carol puts it like this:

> *Away in a manger, no crib for a bed,*
> *the little Lord Jesus laid down His sweet head.*
> *The stars in the sky looked down where He lay,*
> *the little Lord Jesus asleep on the hay.*

Jesus didn't come to earth to have a comfortable life. Jesus came to die for our sins and live in our hearts. On this Christmas Day, have you made room in your heart for Jesus?

THE SUFFERING SERVANT

He was wounded for the wrong things we did.

ISAIAH 53:5 ICB

Things aren't always what they seem.

Jesus was the most wonderful Child ever born—the holy Child of Mary, the divine Son of God. He came on a mission of love and mercy, sent by the Father. An angel announced His coming birth and gave Him His name. The heavenly host praised God together at His birth. An extraordinary star indicated to wise men that He'd been born.

But He came as a Child of the poorest parents, and His earthly life began surrounded by danger. Soon after Jesus was born, King Herod sent soldiers to find and kill Him. Warned by God in a dream, Joseph hurried away from Bethlehem with Mary and the baby Jesus. They went to Egypt until it was safe to return.

The Son of the eternal Father, Jesus also had a human nature. He never sinned, but He experienced suffering. His entire life was one long pathway toward the cross.

Now He is in Heaven, no longer limited by time and space. And someday He will come again—this time in glory—to take us to Himself.

DECEMBER 27

GOD'S WISDOM

How unsearchable are His judgments and His ways past finding out!
ROMANS 11:33

The end of the year is coming, and people are already predicting what the new year will bring. What will the weather be like? What will the school play be? Which team will win the championship? A year from now, most predictions will have missed the target!

The fact is, no one knows the future—except God. We don't even know what will happen next in our own lives. The Bible says, "You do not know what will happen tomorrow" (James 4:14).

And we don't know everything about the world we live in. No doubt scientists will continue to uncover astonishing facts about the universe. But even then, they will know only a tiny amount compared with all there is to know. Only God knows it all, because He created it in the first place.

So what does this mean? It should give us humility before God, and it should give us trust—trust in the God who does know our futures and who works all things for His glory. You can trust all your tomorrows to Him!

PASS ALONG COMFORT

Blessed be the God . . . of all comfort.

2 CORINTHIANS 1:3

One of the apostle Paul's helpers on some of his missionary journeys was named Joseph, but "the apostles called [him] Barnabas (which means Son of Encouragement)" (Acts 4:36 NIV). Barnabas had a gift for finding people who needed a friend to encourage and comfort them. But we can all learn to be like Barnabas.

When we face problems, God comforts us—through the Bible, through the Holy Spirit, and through other Christians. Maybe someone in your family has been sick, but people from your church have come by with food and encouraging words. Maybe some have gone with you to doctor's appointments or sat with your family at the hospital.

Alexander Nowell once said, "God does not comfort us that we may be comforted but that we may be comforters." We are to pass along the comfort with which God has comforted us. This means to find ways to show others that they aren't alone and that God still cares for them.

Look around you. Who do you know who needs comfort or encouragement?

DECEMBER 29

WARNING SIGNS

Use your whole body as an instrument to do
what is right for the glory of God.
ROMANS 6:13 NLT

I n many cities, sirens go off to warn about bad weather so people can go inside and stay safe. A mobile phone beeps to warn that the battery is low and we need to recharge it. At railroad crossings flashing lights warn us to stay off the tracks. Warnings let us know when we need to take some kind of action.

As long as we are in this world, our old sinful ways try to creep back in and turn us away from God. But there are warning signs.

Anytime you see that you haven't been reading your Bible, praying, and being around other Christians—that's a warning. Ask yourself what is going on. Have you been trying to do everything on your own, with no help from the Spirit? Have you let too many other activities fill up your schedule and crowd God out?

When Jesus comes into our hearts, we are to serve Him with our bodies, minds, and spirits. Learn to recognize the warning signs, and with the help of the Holy Spirit, you will be able to "use your whole body as an instrument to do what is right for the glory of God."

GOD'S GIFTS TO US

We have different gifts, according to the grace given us.

ROMANS 12:6 NIV

H ave you ever felt sad when Christmas was over? Maybe you had so much fun you didn't want the holiday to end. Or maybe you felt disappointed—you didn't get a gift you wanted or are already bored with the gifts you got.

God has given gifts to each of us (and I pray we never become bored with them!). The greatest Gift of all, of course, is the gift of His Son. But the Bible also tells us that God gives us *spiritual gifts*—gifts that come from the Holy Spirit's work in our lives.

These gifts of the Spirit include everything from the gift of preaching to the gift of giving with special generosity to the gift of caring for people in need. None of us has every gift, but every Christian has at least one. We are to use them for one purpose: to build up the church—all of Jesus' followers (Ephesians 4:11–12).

Do you wonder which spiritual gifts God has given you? As you grow you will discover more about them. Don't worry about those you don't have. Be content with those God has given you, and use them for the good of others, for His glory.

THE CITY OF GOD

There shall be no night there. . . . And they shall reign forever and ever.
REVELATION 22:5

Many years ago I was visiting the dining room of the United States Senate. As I was speaking with people, one of the senators said, "Billy, we're having a discussion about pessimism and optimism. Are you a pessimist or an optimist?"

I smiled and said, "I'm an optimist." This means I'm usually hopeful that there are good things to come.

The senator asked me why, and I replied, "I've read the last page of the Bible."

The Bible speaks about a heavenly city whose builder and maker is God, where those who have been redeemed will be superior to angels. It speaks of "a pure river of water of life, clear as crystal, proceeding from the throne of God and of the Lamb" (Revelation 22:1). It says, "There shall be no night there: They need no lamp nor light of the sun, for the Lord God gives them light. And they shall reign forever and ever" (v. 5).

You have had both joys and disappointments this year. Now look forward to the new year and every year after that until Jesus comes back. Even more, look forward to Heaven. "Be patient and stand firm, because the Lord's coming is near" (James 5:8 NIV).

READING THE BIBLE

The Bible is *the* most important book you will ever read. It is God's plan for your life. In the Bible, God tells you how to love Him and how to love others. He tells you what is right and what is wrong. And most important of all, He tells you how to get to Heaven. Because the Bible is so important, it's a good idea to read something from it every day.

Try one of these reading plans to help you get started. Put a check next to each one as you read it. "30 Days with Jesus" walks you through the life of Jesus, telling of the things He did and taught while He was here on earth. "90 Days Through the Bible" gives you all the major happenings of the Old and New Testaments, beginning with the Creation in Genesis and going all the way through to Revelation.

30 DAYS WITH JESUS

1. John 1:1–51 _____
2. Luke 2:1–52 _____
3. Mark 1:1–11 _____
4. Luke 4:1–44 _____
5. John 3:1–36 _____
6. Luke 5:1–39 _____

1. Genesis 1:1–2:3 _____

2. Genesis 3:1–24 _____

3. Genesis 6:9–7:24 _____

4. Genesis 8:1–9:17 _____

5. Genesis 17:1–22 _____

6. Genesis 22:1–19 _____

7. Genesis 25:19–34 _____

8. Genesis 27:1–28:9 _____

9. Genesis 37:1–36 _____

10. Genesis 41:1–57 _____

11. Genesis 45:1–28 _____

12. Exodus 1:8–2:15 _____

13. Exodus 3:1–4:17 _____

14. Exodus 5:1–6:13 _____

15. Exodus 12:1–42 _____

16. Exodus 13:17–14:31 _____

17. Exodus 20:1–21 _____

18. Numbers 13:1–33 _____

19. Joshua 2:1–24 _____

20. Joshua 6:1–27 _____

21. Judges 16:4–31 _____

22. 1 Samuel 1:1–28 _____

23. 1 Samuel 3:1–21 _____

24. 1 Samuel 10:1–27 _____

25. 1 Samuel 16:1–13 _____

26. 1 Samuel 17:1–58 _____

27. 1 Samuel 24:1–22 _____

28. 2 Samuel 11:1–12:25 _____

29. 1 Kings 3:1–28 _____

30. 1 Kings 17:8–24 _____

31. 1 Kings 18:1–46 _____

32. 2 Kings 2:1–18 _____

33. 2 Kings 4:8–37 _____

34. 2 Chronicles 35:20–36:23 _____

35. Esther 2:1–23 _____

36. Esther 6:1–8:8 _____

37. Job 1:1–2:13; 42:1–17 _____

38. Psalm 23:1–6 _____

39. Psalm 51:1–19 _____

40. Psalm 100:1–5 _____

41. Psalm 121:1–8 _____

42. Psalm 145:1–21 _____

43. Proverbs 4:1–27 _____

44. Ecclesiastes 11:9–12:14 _____

45. Isaiah 53:1–12 _____

46. Daniel 1:1–21 _____

47. Daniel 3:1–30 _____

48. Daniel 6:1–28 _____

49. Jonah 1:1–4:11 _____

50. Matthew 1:18–2:23 _____

51. Matthew 5:1–16; 6:1–7:12 _____

52. Matthew 14:13–36 _____

53. Matthew 21:1–17 _____

54. Matthew 26:47–75 _____

55. Matthew 27:15–66 _____

56. Matthew 28:1–20 _____

57. Mark 1:1–20 _____

58. Mark 4:1–20 _____

59. Luke 1:26–56; 2:1–20 _____

60. Luke 10:25–42; 14:25–35 _____

61. Luke 15:1–32 _____

62. Luke 22:1–23 _____

63. Luke 24:13–53 _____

64. John 1:1–18 _____

65. John 3:1–21 _____

66. John 4:1–42 _____

67. John 8:1–11 _____

68. John 11:1–44 _____

69. John 14:1–31 _____

70. Acts 1:1–11 _____

71. Acts 2:1–47 _____

72. Acts 8:26–40 _____

73. Acts 9:1–31 _____

74. Acts 11:1–18 _____

75. Acts 16:11–40 _____

76. Romans 3:1–31 _____

77. Romans 8:1–39 _____

78. Romans 12:1–21 _____

79. 1 Corinthians 13:1–13 _____

80. 1 Corinthians 15:1–58 _____

81. Ephesians 2:1–22; 6:10–20 _____

82. Philippians 3:1–4:9 _____

83. Colossians 3:1–4:1 _____

84. 1 Thessalonians 4:1–18 _____

85. Hebrews 11:1–40 _____

86. James 1:1–27 _____

87. James 3:1–18 _____

88. 1 Peter 1:3–25 _____

89. 1 John 1:1–2:17 _____

90. Revelation 21:1–22:21 _____

_____

_____

_____

_____

_____

_____

_____

_____

JOURNALING

The same devotions that encourage your children will comfort you each day of the year.

LASTING, BIBLICAL HOPE CAN BE YOURS WITH THIS timeless classic. Every day, fill your heart and mind with the presence and fullness of God's grace and power in your life. Your soul will be blessed and God's everlasting hope will remain at the center of all that you do.

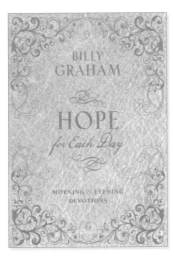

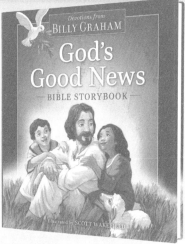